Picking

Butter Beans

Picking Butter Beans

By Steven D. Davis

Minneapolis

This book is a work of fiction. The characters, incidents, and dialogue are drawn from the author's imagination and are not to be construed as real. Any resemblance to actual events or persons, living or dead, is entirely coincidental.

Cover Illustration by Anthony Palumbo

Published by

Waldman & Company, Inc., an imprint of

Bookmen Media Group, Inc
331 Main Street South
Rice Lake, WI 54868
www.bookmenmediagroup.com

Ordering Information:
Quantity sales. Special discounts are available on quantity purchases by corporations, associations, and others. For details, contact the publisher at the address above.

Softcover edition ISBN 978-0-9911340-0-7
E-book edition ISBN 978-0-9911340-1-4

First Edition

Library of Congress Presassigned Control Number   2013943184

Manufactured in the United States of America
18 17 16 15 14 13 / 6 5 4 3 2 1

For Fisher and Seb

and

Mary Helen Pressley Campbell

May God tenderly rest you
in the arms of your mom and dad.
I love you to the moon and back.

— Papi

"Life is not measured by the number of breaths we take,

but by the number of moments that take our breath away."

Anonymous

Foreword

Have you ever met someone you instantly liked? Perhaps you couldn't put your finger on it, but you knew that you just liked them? This feeling was confirmed about Steve Davis when he inquired about the possibility of taking two of our boys to one of his favorite places on earth, the Snake River, for a once in a lifetime fishing trip.

We went with Steve to The Lodge at Palisades Creek, and true to his word, two young men who live at Big Oak Ranch—a home for orphaned, abused, neglected, and homeless children—had the trip of a lifetime on the famous Snake River.

On the trip, Steve shared childhood stories about growing up in Texas and his growing passion to make others a priority. At first I was enamored with his amiable personality and joy for life, but later, I found out that there was so much more to this man. Steve's shift in his life's purpose was so evident that I immediately became a huge fan.

At the end of the week, I was humbled when he asked if I would write the foreword for this book, Picking Butter Beans. My friends will tell you I'm not one to jump on a request like this, but I couldn't wait to read this book after watching this man interact with two boys who had endured a tough beginning.

When you read this book, I promise you will cheer, be sad, laugh, grow angry, feel relief, and empathize with a young man who carried around a deep secret no one knew about.

All of us have secrets we have to deal with in this journey called life. This story provides tremendous encouragement for us all to move forward with our lives.

So many people are paralyzed with shame and guilt that are clearly not of their choosing. Like young Jake Travis, they just can't shake that burning desire to "make the bad dreams go away" nor are they able to recognize and tell themselves this basic truth about childhood abuse: "It wasn't my fault."

So many people go through life seeking ways to break free of the heavy weight of bondage to the past. They cannot stop the seemingly endless cycle of "digging in the grave of skeletons."

If you are trying to drive down the road of life looking in the rear view mirror, I can guarantee you that you will eventually wreck—it's just a matter of time. The main character in this novel, Jake Travis, allowed an empathetic friend named Mel to enter his life, and she taught Jake how to look out the windshield of life and not focus on the rear view mirror. He no longer had to experience life as he thought it was supposed to be: "a life that was one large secret."

There's a verse in the Bible that says, "You shall know the truth and the truth shall make you free."

Discover as you read what it took to be free and learn how a young man gained that freedom we all so desperately seek.

John Croyle

About John Croyle

John played on the University of Alabama's 1973 National Championship football team, as a defensive-end for the legendary Coach Paul "Bear" Bryant. At 19, John felt he had been given a gift to work with young people. On the advice of Coach Bryant, John declined opportunities for professional football to pursue his dream of creating the best children's home in America.

In 1974, he founded Big Oak Ranch, a home for orphaned, abused, neglected, and homeless children, in Gadsden, Alabama. Since then, more than 1,800 children have called Big Oak Ranch home. In addition to his work on-site at the Ranch, John speaks across the Southeast at 75-plus events annually. Events range from corporate to motivational to Christian-based organizational events.

Learning a lifetime of lessons by helping to raise more than 1,800 children, John continues to pursue his vision to help people everywhere become better parents.

Preface

April 4, 2006

As she finished the last page of the journal, a tear bled down her cheek. Dr. Mel Allen didn't know if it was the story she read or the last words staring back at her.

"The End."

The constant drip of morphine tricked her emotions and held her body in check. But somehow, the words on these pages deserved a response.

Despite her weakened condition, she felt relief and gave a deep sigh. Even that took more energy than she expected.

She slowly closed the binding and held the wrinkled pages tight against her chest. Those gathered in the room were still, the silence broken only by the hum of the machines connecting her to life.

Her family and friends moved about the small room quietly, whispering when words needed to be spoken. Doors opened and closed with a hush. She felt the breeze from the open window. The smells of spring and pollen flooded her senses.

Her favorite time. April.

Hospice moved into their suburban home a few days before and converted her quaint bedroom into a make-shift hospital room. A single room where goodbyes were spoken to family and friends. A private setting for final embraces of two people still in love. It was her last room, the one she would never leave.

She turned to her husband who sat beside her solemnly and pointed to a small wicker basket of addressed envelopes. "Paul, please make sure they all get their notes," she pleaded. "And, don't send Jake's through the post. Deliver it personally for me."

He simply nodded, and before he could say anything, the nurse stepped to the IV bag hanging near Mel's bed.

"The dose is being increased now. It will take a few minutes, but it will help you relax, and you will not feel anxious." She paused and tapped the port with her finger. "I promise."

When the nurse stepped away, Paul leaned over, careful of the lines and needles, and whispered in her ear, "No worries, baby. I'll deliver them all." He fought his own tears, and as she closed her eyes, he sighed, "I love you, Mel."

And then she was gone.

CHAPTER ONE

The Candy Jar

(July 10, 2005)

MUD HOLES, rusty lawnmowers, and empty beer cans littered the gravel driveway. The sign read "Bert's Smokehouse and Small Engine Repair." I pulled my rental between two dented, camouflaged, pickup trucks and shut the engine off. The screen door dangling from its hinges and the aroma of bacon dribbling from within the shack reminded me of the days when my dad and I would come here for lunch. As I entered, the corner jukebox cranked out some song about chewing gum. "You ain't nuthin' but a chiclet on the bottom of my shoe." Must be a big hit; the two youngsters snuggling in the dark corner seemed to know the words.

"Howdy," the waitress yelled, "come on in. Sit anywhere you like, honey. Lunch crowd left an hour ago. Brisket's all gone. Be there in a spot."

I wandered to a corner booth near the window, tested the table top to see if it was wobbly and slid in. Glancing around, I wrestled a handful of napkins from the tin dispenser and dipped below to steady the base. It was almost there when the waitress snapped me back to attention. My head bounced up.

"Do you wanna eat, get drunk, or just fool around?" she barked, leaning into the booth, so that her name tag dangled in front of my eyes. "Hank," it read. She was tall, slim, and wore a pink top, with skinny jeans. The small apron tied around her waist was stained and filled with pens and plastic forks.

"That's smokehouse humor, honey. It's too early to fool around. But I get off at 6:00, just in case you wonderin'." She smiled.

I cleared my throat and squinted at the menu scrawled across the chalkboard posted above the bar. "Can I get a chopped beef sandwich and a Miller Lite?"

"Sure, honey," Hank drawled.

"And do you think there might be a steady table in here?" I asked, wiggling the top. "See?"

Hank took a quick look around. "Well... nope, but knock yourself out trying. You might get lucky ... but I seriously doubt it. This place is held together by my bubbly personality and a rigid cash-only policy."

She watched me as I worked the pedestal over the napkins. Finally, I looked up and smiled. "There ... much better."

"Good job, cowboy. Now...do you want the spicy sauce, the tangy red sauce, the habanera green with chili peppers, the urban white boy or just regular?" Hank asked.

"Just regular, I guess." I glanced over at the two kids, now enjoying a lingering kiss.

"Not happening—completely sold out of regular," she said, tapping her pen against her cheek.

"Oh...OK. How about the urban white boy?" I asked. "Is that any good?"

"That's my personal fave. A bit spicy, but you might enjoy livin' on the edge," she said, pulling a fly swatter from her skinny jeans pocket.

I watched her eyes dart around and asked. "So, how long have you been out of the regular sauce?"

"Going on two years now," she answered, slapping the edge of the table. "Bingo—been after that little sucker since daylight." She wiped the table with a dingy dish rag. It didn't help much. "Honey, you still want that sauce on the side, right?"

Hank moved like a foreman way behind schedule, so before I could answer, she was back with my beer.

"Cowboy, you sure are dressed up and all and you look familiar. But I gotta say—you must not be from around here. We don't see many suits in Legit, at least the kind made out of cloth," she said. "You ain't on the T.V. or something, are ya?" She cocked her head sideways. "Wait—don't tell me—Health Department. You took Rawley's place down at the county?"

"No, uh … not sure what you're talking about. Who's Rawley?" I said, sipping my beer.

"Rawley used to be our health inspector—for ages," she said. "We had a thing for a while—well … just a weekend really."

"Wow, I'm sorry to hear that," I said, pulling some sanitary wipes from my pocket and scrubbing my space. "Sounds like you guys were really close."

"Yeah … well, I still tear up a bit when I think about him." She pulled up a chair and took a seat. "So, tell me, what brings a 'suit' like you to this pothole little town?"

"Family," I said. "Just back for a quick visit." I looked up at her. She was not unattractive in an East Texas sort of way. Lose the pink shades in her hair and the barb wire tattoo—she could be … pretty. "What's with the name tag? Hank?"

Hank glanced down at her badge and grinned. "Well, I was born at the butt-end of a long line of girls. Five to be exact. Daddy was so flustered by all the women bossing him around. He just wanted a boy in a bad way—named me Henrietta. Since I was a little girl, he called me Hank. Guess it stuck."

"Guess so. Thanks, Hank. I'm Jake."

Hank stuck out her right hand. "Nice to meet ya, Jake." Her grip spoke of hard work and long hours.

"Back in a holler with your order, honey." She stood and yelled...
"Urban boy...on the side." As she marched away, I watched her stick her head into the kitchen. "Lloyd, we got an urban boy sittin' out here." She glanced back at me. "Wearing a suit and tie."

I heard a deep voice deep inside the kitchen ask. "Is he...county?"

"Says no. I believe him." She half-glanced back to my table—just to make sure.

I straightened my tie, picked up the local paper, and began to browse through the eight pages of news. Tommy Kildare killed a rattlesnake down by Trout Creek. Billy Bonds was running for City Council. There was a campaign for a new red light down by the high school, and Sheila Campbell was getting married for the third time.

Gripping.

Hank appeared within minutes juggling a beef barbeque sandwich on day-old white bread. The plate was dressed with a stale dill pickle and a cup of red sauce. She slid the plate in front of me, tossed a plastic fork and knife on the table, and pulled a cold beer from her apron.

"Honey, I reckoned you for at least two beers. Hope I ain't being too forward," she said, setting the beer down in front of me.

"Not at all, Hank. Thanks. You know, I used to eat here as a kid. It really hasn't changed much in thirty years. Do you still have the big round candy jar on the counter next to the cash register? Bert used to let me reach in for a free piece when I was little. My brother broke a tooth on candy from that jar."

Lifting the hot sandwich, I took a long bite and washed it down.

"Well, you know, Bert's been dead for a hundred years, but I can tell ya, there ain't nothing free in this place but yesterday's gossip." Hank peeped over my shoulder. "Hold that thought. Be back in two." She hustled to the kids in the corner and delivered their tab, saying something about a hotel room. Hank waited for them to pay, counted the cash and sat back down beside me. "So, you were sayin'."

I smiled. "Well, you and Lloyd seem a bit concerned about the county health inspector. What's the deal?" I was killing off my sandwich and reaching for my pickle.

"Oh…nothing really. They shut us down last month and just between us girls, we're still shut down. Lloyd ripped the stamp off the door early this morning, claiming he's got a right to make a livin'. Texas is a right to work state, he says. Anyways, we had over twelve health violations. Can you believe that? Twelve! We usually don't have more than nine, maybe ten, at the most, but twelve is a really big number."

I cleared my throat and studied my empty plate. "What type of violations?"

She rolled her eyes. "Little things. Just stupid things. Nit-picky…if you ask me."

"Not sure I understand," I said, pushing my plate away and pulling at my collar. I could feel my heart rate rising. "What do you mean… little things?"

"Let's see. We got carded for cleanliness, meat separation, and refrigeration. Sure, our refrigerator broke down. Wasn't our fault! Also, Lloyd refuses to wear a hair net, and we got busted big time for animals in the kitchen—apparently that's a big no-no."

"Animals…like a dog or horse?"

Hank stood and laughed. "You're silly. Rodents . . . like in water rats. They're everywhere. Lloyd found two in the traps this morning. They're big and mean." She paused a second and lowered her voice.

"Listen, we have a band tonight. Really good one. Starts at 8:00. Why don't you come back out? I'll scoot you around the dance floor. I bet, if you lose that tie and jacket, swallow a valium or two, you might relax."

"Geez, Hank, that's an offer hard to pass up, but I don't see myself 'scooting' anywhere—particularly on a dance floor—even with the help of medication. But, thanks all the same—I won't be spending the night, anyway. I have a late flight out of Houston."

"Fair enough—maybe next time, pretty boy." She gave me an obvious wink and placed the check on the table.

Henrietta.

శ్రీ

I pointed the bumper north and noticed that the gas gauge was lit. A few miles later, I pulled under a rickety green canopy—Gerald's Gas & Tire. After killing the engine, I stepped out and watched a lanky man shuffle from the garage bay pushing an empty dolly. The old man wore dirty overalls, and his cap backward on his head. He wiped his greasy hands with an oil rag and then dabbed at his forehead.

"Howdy." The old man greeted me. Looking down at my front tires he said, "Tires look good—which means you need gas."

"Fill 'er up." I walked around the car to meet him. "Regular unleaded."

"Name's Gerald—own the place." He extended his hand.

"I'm Jake...nice to meet you, Gerald." He pulled open the gas cap and inserted the nozzle.

"You smell like you just had lunch down at Bert's."

I lowered my jaw and sniffed.

"County shut 'em down...oh...month ago now," Gerald reported. "Twelve violations is what the rumors say. That's a big number, you know...twelve."

I reached into the back seat, retrieved my jacket from the hanger, and gave it a sniff. No mistaking that smell. I tossed the jacket on the rear seat and shut the door. "Do you have a restroom?"

Gerald nodded his head toward the back. "Yep, around back. Don't need a key, but watch the flusher, it's a bit cantankerous," he said, replacing the nozzle on the tank.

When I returned, he stood at the cash register. "Cash or credit?"

I pushed a card to him.

"Might have to burn that nice jacket, son… 'less you want to attract a herd of hounds. You could try the cleaners, but they send it to the next county for processing. Could take a couple of days to get it back," advised Gerald as he slid the card through the register. "Their service ain't the best around, and they do have a tendency to lose things…just so you know."

I nodded my thanks. "I know Legit is a bit sketchy for accommodations, but any suggestions?" I asked. "The last time I stayed at a motel in Legit, I had to fight the rats for my blanket."

The old man smiled and handed back my card with a receipt. "Where do you want to end up, son?"

"I have business here in Legit, but maybe as far as Roganville…just a few miles north of here."

"Hotels are kinda scarce in these parts. Motel 96 is located right off this road…'bout four miles north of town, but if you don't mind driving a bit further, the Clyburn Bed and Breakfast is nice. Good food. Nice Christian folk."

"How far?"

"Ten miles north of Legit…maybe less."

He walked me out to my car, giving me turn by turn directions to the Clyburn. "If you get to the Whataburger—you've gone too far."

"I grew up in this part of Texas. Ashamed to say, it's been years since I visited. But, it sure has changed," I said. "This area was once a thriving community. What happened?"

Gerald sighed. "Little spots like Legit hang on by a thread. Time's always in a hurry and is often unforgiving in its desire to move on—and quickly. Twenty years ago, I had three men working for me, and we still couldn't keep up with the demand. Today, we got boarded windows, potholes, and feral dogs." He shook his head. "Time left here years ago, and nobody noticed."

We said our goodbyes, and I pulled back onto highway 96. As I drove, dirt roads seemed to vanish into the shady Texas pines, while thinly paved asphalt roads begged for a county budget. By the look of things, I suspected my hometown now had more tattoos than transmissions. Gerald was right. Time left years ago—nobody noticed.

Hemmed in by the East Texas Big Thicket, the Alabama Coushatta Indian Reservation and the Louisiana border, Legit's genetic tree sprang only a few limbs. The townsfolk had a limited yet entertaining heritage. There were the born-and-raised East Texas toothless, the Irish, one Hispanic family, the Cajuns from New Orleans, a covey of Pentecostals, and a few people from Oklahoma. Those Sooners and their double-wides snuck into town one weekend and never left. Word had it they were running from the law. If I were running from the law, Legit, Texas would be the first place I would crawl into and hide. Not much happened and when it did, not much happened.

Plenty of my relatives still lived in Legit, including my mom and dad, but I kept my rental pushing north, driving another twenty miles. I had my reasons for the diversion—avoiding family stood near the top. Most of my class friends escaped Legit the weekend after graduation. My little brother and sister toyed with idea of sticking around, but came to their senses after school.

After topping the big hill outside the county line, I flew past the Clyburn Bed and Breakfast. I made a quick about turn and pulled in. The sign out in front of the white, clapboard house boasted of four bedrooms and a bath. From the road, it looked neatly kept. Large pines and spent azaleas covered the grounds. A narrow colorful garden lined the front of the building. Lantana, Zinnia and Tyler Roses were scattered along the sidewalk. The wide dirt parking lot was fenced and cluttered with dusty cars, a few with tags from faraway places, like Arkansas. I parked and grabbed my bag.

Resembling a sales lady from the Home Shopping Network, the hostess at the counter greeted me with a wide toothy smile. Her large frame dwarfed the picture of Jesus hanging behind her.

"Sir, Jesus is surely blessing you today," the woman declared. She wore a bright blue flower-print dress and seemed particularly proud of the cherry red lipstick.

"We have a single bed available. You know, it's Magnolia Festival week, so things are hopping around here like a bug hatch on Friday night. Busy, busy, busy," she boasted. "The room ain't got a T.V., but you can watch it downstairs in the living room. Harold—that's my husband—just bought a brand new wide screen. It's what they call, HD. You ever heard of that? Prettiest thing I ever did see." She paused, leaned into the counter and whispered, "Likely made in China or Japan. One of them foreign places…you know."

She pulled a piece of paper from a drawer and slid it across at me and continued. "There ain't no smokin', cussin' or drinkin'. We're all Baptist here and don't take our Bible verses lightly. No sir."

When she took a breath, I asked. "What about the bathroom? Is there a bathroom attached to the single bed without the T.V. where there's no smoking or drinking?" I asked.

She handed me a skeleton key chained to a complete King James Version of the New Testament. "The bathroom is at the end of the hallway—third floor, just three doors down from your room." The smile quickly disappeared into her jowls, and she cleared her throat. "Don't forget, there's no cussin'…and no elevator," she said.

"What's this?" I asked, trying to stuff the Bible key chain into my suit jacket.

"Can't have you losing the key, plus you might want to have some reading material. I personally recommend the book of John," she said, revealing teeth traced with lipstick. "Bless you, Mr. Jacob Travis. May Jesus be with you tonight." She straightened her long skirt, lifted her double chin, and waited for me to leave.

"Will you send Jesus his part of the bill?" I asked, lifting my bag to my shoulder. I gave her a quick wink, said thank you and disappeared into a hallway cluttered with small tables bearing large colorful vases. Managing the key and the lock, I entered the tiny attic room. The yellow wallpaper and blue drapes spoke of Laura Ashley and high tea. Flowers...everywhere.

My head began to throb.

I parked my things in the corner, tossed water and cologne on my face and glanced around for Jesus. I snatched my car keys and squeezed down the narrow stairway to escape before my head exploded.

I had a funeral to attend.

CHAPTER TWO

Visitation

SMELLING LESS LIKE BERT'S and more like Polo, I pulled back out on the highway and drove the few miles to Legit.

The last time I visited home, my cousin, Taterbug, shamed me into investing in his worm farm. A great marketer, Taterbug named a run-down converted gas station "Worm Your Way In." It took him six months to discover that selling the idea was easier than actually raising the worms. Rumors speak of a new business venture: raising catfish. And I want none of it. For this reason, I kept my return quiet.

The purpose of my visit became painfully real as I approached the First Baptist Church. The red brick building was notably perched on the corner of Main and Chesterfield. I pulled into a vacant parking spot across the street and sat with the engine idling. As usual, I was early. A few cars and pick-up trucks lined Main Street. Others made the journey as well. Lots of people will make the trip as a sign of respect and honor. I suspected the sanctuary would be packed with mourners. It always was.

In East Texas, there are two major social events: high school football games, and funeral visitations. No one gets buried properly until after the visitation, but it had little to do with burying the dead and more to do with feeding the living.

The Blues Club formed a close-knit group of elderly women who secretly used visitations as cook-offs. If it could be fried in fat-back, stuffed into casing, baked or barbequed, it would be found on the table. They controlled visitations in Legit like the mob did Vegas. Hattie Mitchell served as President Emeritus of the Blues. She organized a communication system that rivaled Google's.

Mrs. Mitchell taught English during my years in high school. With her wide, red pen in constant need of refills, she scribbled relentlessly on our papers. She wrote words like "mercy" and "apoplexy" —a more difficult grade to decipher—to grade papers. My grades were never in question. She only wrote the word "Jesus" on my assignments.

A few cars pulled up to the back of the church, as I watched the activity move in and out of the red brick building. Several women dismounted their pick-up trucks and filed into the building balancing plates and platters. I reached down to switch the engine off, and sat fiddling with the keys.

I thought after all of the years, did it really matter that I was here? Would it help the dead? Would it hurt the living?

I lowered my car window, sat back, and closed my eyes—a million sights and sounds of my past pulled at my senses. The look of a freshly cut hay field, as the dew dried. The sound of my granny's voice booming from the butter bean patch. My dad banging the skillet at daybreak. Mom's curly hair bouncing as she shucked corn on the porch. I thought about how time lacked the capacity to heal all my wounds—that there are things some people never really stop paying for. I thought about how the energy that pulled me through my darkest hours tended to consist of short moments filled with few words, often spoken by the most unexpected individual.

I'm not sure the answers I needed were here … this day … but the memories certainly were.

CHAPTER THREE

A Traveling Man (1964)

"GRANNY... I'M COMING!" I yelled. "I'm in the outhouse."
Geez, can't a guy even take a whiz in peace, I thought.

My granny had one volume...loud. "Jake, you and me gotta lot of beans to pick out here. Where are you?" Her hearing left years ago. I guess she thought I lost mine as well.

"Grab your bucket, boy, and get out here. Daylight's burning fast."

I stood in the outhouse for a couple of minutes longer, buying time.

"Quit wasting time. I know you're not in there peeing," she said, resting her hands on her wide hips.

I glanced around. There were peep holes in this place large enough to drive a tractor through. Her ears may be gone, but she can see two squirrels fighting over an acorn a mile away.

"Granny, how do you know that?" I asked.

"Trust me, Jake. Granny knows everything."

That's what scared me to death.

"Okay. Okay. I'm coming," I said, lifting my head to the ceiling and yelling. "I think I might have a stomach ache!"

As a nine-year-old, I learned that my body was not built to be a farmer. Farmers went to bed when it was light out and woke when it was dark, and they bantered endlessly about the weather. Not me. A couple of years ago, I wanted to be a cowboy, roaming the countryside ridding the world of nasty gunslingers—to ride my palomino horse. All I needed was a six shooter, some bullets, and maybe a white cowboy hat…and, of course, a ticket out.

Today, I want to be a traveling man. I figured that traveling the world would keep me out of the garden, pulling weeds, pushing a plow or working the dusty rows with a hoe. I would be out there, wherever that was. Making things happen, whatever that meant.

Often, my granny came over to work in our garden, and she insisted that I work beside her. Every step. At that age, I didn't have all of my teeth, but I would rather gum my food for the rest of my life than work in a garden. Garden work left me bent and sore and meant I couldn't climb a tree or fry fire ants with a magnifying glass. It took time away from shooting beer cans with my Daisy BB gun or fishing for crappie over at Lumpkin's pond.

My granny was as sturdy as the pine trees that lined our county and a real task master. Once, I winced a bit feigning a serious spinal problem as I picked up my red plastic bucket, limping all the way to the garden. That didn't seem to buy much attention from her. Kicking at dirt clumps seemed to always raise the bar a bit. With Granny, no one ever really knew which button to push. So, I decided to push them all today.

As I stepped out of the outhouse, Granny was standing not ten feet away from me. "You must have a bladder the size of Dallas. Now, if you are done hiding in the toilet, maybe we can get some work done," she said. "Come on. It's a great day to be out picking beans and milking cows. And why are you yelling at Granny? You think I'm hard of hearing or something?"

"No ma'am. Just not feeling real good today," I said, fumbling with my zipper.

"Well, I've got some of my sick balm in the icebox. Do you want me to run and fetch it for you? Won't take but a second," she said.

Granny could sense my lack of enthusiasm. With most grandparents, you could complain of a stomach ache and within minutes, they'd have you strapped to a gurney at the county hospital. Not Granny—she had this stinky balm handkerchief that smelled of old catfish baking in the Texas sun. If she strapped that thing around my neck, I'd really be sick.

Granny wore her long, silver hair in a beehive. Her callused hands spoke of life on the farm. Backwoods Baptist religious roots contributed to her stern demeanor. Her life had been rough for as long as she could remember—the Depression, multiple wars, and Grandpa. I always suspected, however, that Grandpa put the white in her hair. I do know Granny put the lump on Grandpa's head, clobbering him with a fifth of whiskey. She never liked his drinking or his cussing.

Granny's wardrobe was simple: three plaid dresses—two for working the farm and one for the House of the Lord. Her eyes were deep set and blue, and her weathered face never saw a hint of makeup. Still, I thought she was beautiful. She was my granny, and being her first grandchild, I always thought she loved me most. Many years lapsed before I understood why.

"Jake, tell me something, young man. What do you want to be when you grow up big?" she asked, grabbing two large pails full to the brim with fresh milk.

"Ain't gonna be a farmer, that's for sure," I said, reaching down for a large rock to throw against the barn door.

"Really now? You know farming is a pretty important job."

"How's that?" I asked, finding another stone to whirl at the old barn.

"You like to eat, don't ya?"

"Yeah…guess so."

She paused and set her milk buckets down and said, "Well then, where do you think all the food comes from that you eat?"

"The farm," I answered, shaking my head. "But I want to travel around the world, Granny. See things. Do stuff. I want to fly in a plane. Ride in a car with air-conditioning."

"You could stay right here with me," she said. "I'd be willing to pay you high cotton to rub my corns."

"Granny, I ain't gonna rub your feet for money." I thought about it. "Well, how much money?"

"A nickel a corn," she said. "That's a lot of money to just rub a corn."

I thought hard about that and did some quick calculations. I looked down at her feet—rough and ugly.

"Granny," I said, "I think I'll pass on the corn offer…but thanks all the same."

"So 'iffin you ain't gonna be a farmer or a corn-rubber, what're you gonna be?"

"A traveling man."

"A traveling man?" she repeated. "Well, how you gonna make money? What're you gonna eat? Where will you live?"

"I don't have it all figured out just yet, Granny. Heck, I'm only nine years old. Maybe I can sell something, like that fat man with the wig who comes to our house. He's real nice, and Momma always lets him vacuum the floors. She gives him cookies and iced tea."

"Well, if you want to be a traveling salesman, you better be fast on your feet. You know what I mean?" She lifted her buckets and quickened her pace.

"Yeah, I guess," I said, noticing she was beginning to leave me.

"Because if you ain't fast on your feet—the only thing you gonna eat is dust…my dust." Granny gave me a big smile and pointed to the garden. It was less than fifty yards away. "One, two, … three!" She gave me a couple of steps lead, but it didn't matter—she outran me by a nose while carrying two buckets of milk, spilling nary a drop. My granny couldn't hear a tractor tire explode, but she could run like the wind.

When we reached the end of the barn, Granny smiled at me. I smiled back. She grabbed me and hugged me tight. "I love you my little man, and if you want to wear a suit and get tossed out of folks homes at night, be the very best you can. Work hard at it. But remember…life's a stretch more than tea and cookies."

She paused and glanced up at the sky. "Jake, the weatherman is giving out storms later today. We don't have much time before the clouds open up."

"All right, but I still ain't gonna be no farmer man," I said, kicking at a dirt clump at the end of the garden.

"You take the butter beans, and I'll start over here on the okra," she said, pouring milk into a stainless steel container.

I stood there peering down at the straight narrow rows of the garden. They seemed to stretch from my backyard to downtown Legit. My dad always plowed perfectly straight rows, which created an optical illusion. The moist heat was baking my head like a furnace. The mild breeze disappeared as I placed my stool in the middle of the row. I looked up into the sky, and sure enough, the sun was bouncing in and out of the thick clouds. Rain.

Giving out storms.

I shook my head and sighed, fearing this farm would be my life forever. I toiled my way down the row, picking and dreaming at each bushy plant. I dreamed of what I would do when I got my first car. What would that be? Where would it take me? I also had other dreams. Unpleasant ones. I stood there in the dusty row wondering if Granny would understand those dreams and help make them go away.

Shaking my head to rid those thoughts, I glanced over to the barn.

Would I see the world through the windshield of our plow tractor? I hoped not. I wasn't sure it would make it to the main road.

"Jake!" Granny yelled. "I'm watching you."

"Okay," I kicked my bucket down the row.

CHAPTER FOUR

Mrs. Poodie's Flower Shop

THOUGH THINGS WERE SLOW IN LEGIT, Texas, what people overheard in conversations usually made up for it. Rumors usually started at the whittling bench on Main Street. True or not. It's one of the best places to eavesdrop on what might be happening in the neighboring towns. One of my fondest memories was spending time with my dad kicking cans down Main, on the way to the bench.

Every Saturday morning, we rose early and did our chores. Around lunch time, Dad washed up and loaded the truck for the five-mile drive into town, blazing a trail to Jones' Feed Store to pick up supplies and discuss the weather forecast for the next hundred years. Typically, I selected a Campbell's can from the nearest trash barrel and kicked it down to the whittling bench. But on this particular Saturday, I took a side trip over to Mrs. Poodie's Flower Shop. Think proms, funerals, and beauty pageants—Legit had more than its share.

Gladys Poodie owned the only solvent flower shop in town; rumor had it she owned interest in half of Legit. A war bride, Mrs. Poodie "still wears her military shoes from the Big War," Momma would tell my dad. Momma didn't shop in her store very often.

Mrs. Poodie was married to the principal of my school. Tall and lean with a beaked nose and hefty breast, she was known about town as a smart, hard-nosed entrepreneur. Those she crossed, called her the Jezebel. I didn't know what an entrepreneur was, so I asked my mom one afternoon while she was shelling beans on the back porch.

"Momma?"

"Yes, Jakey. What's on your mind?" She could shell beans, drink coffee and skin a chicken all at once.

"Well ... I've been watching Mr. Cronkite on the news, and our army's bombing that place called 'Nam."

"Does that worry you, Jakey?" she asked, tossing freshly shelled beans into a bucket of ice water.

"A little, I guess. But what if that 'Nam man gets a plane and tries to bomb Legit?" I asked.

Mom paused her bean shucking and turned to face me. "Honey, the last place on earth they would bomb would be this little hole in the road. Don't worry so much about that, okay?"

"Would they bomb our house ... you think?"

"No, Jake. They don't know where we live."

"What about the Chat & Chew?"

"Well, if they did, it would be the biggest grease fire this side of New York City. Don't worry so much, honey." Mom turned back to her bucket of beans and resumed shelling.

"Okay."

We sat in silence for a few moments, and then I grabbed a fly swatter. I chased bugs around the porch for a while. I killed a few, missed a bunch, and sat back down. Avoiding my bucket of butter beans, I grabbed my baseball and studied the stitching, turning the ball over and over in my hand. I stood and pretended to wind up my fast ball.

"Momma?"

"Yes, honey."

"What's a non-trepreneur?"

Her forehead wrinkled as she looked over to my untouched bucket of beans.

"Jake, do you mean entrepreneur?" she asked, nudging my bucket closer to my rocking chair with her foot.

"I think so."

"Son, those beans ain't gonna shell themselves, you know. Put that ball down, it's getting late."

About that time, Dad stepped onto the porch. To me, he was the smartest man on the planet, and he reminded me of that fact all the time. He spit a wad of Red Man into the grass and placed his hands on his hips. "Jake, an entrepreneur is someone who sleeps their way to the top." He let go of another long spit and gave Momma a grin, grabbing an empty pail and quickly setting off for the garden.

I could tell Momma didn't take to his definition by the look she shot him. It was lost on Dad's rear-end as he hustled away.

"Jake, why do you want to know?" she asked. "You thinking about becoming an entrepreneur?"

"Maybe someday. The old men down on the bench say Mrs. Poodie is one of those."

Momma stopped shelling and looked over at me. She was debating what to say. "An entrepreneur is typically someone who invests money in a business with the prospect of that investment paying back more money in the future. But...given that your reference is to Mrs. Poodie, I think your daddy's definition is spot on."

I could end up owning half of Legit; all I needed was more sleep, I thought.

Mrs. Poodie didn't have kids of her own, so her tolerance level was on the low end of none. When my buddies and I visited her shop, she would track us like a blood hound after a T-bone.

This sunny morning, I slipped inside unnoticed, hidden behind a couple of large ladies searching for the perfect hand-painted vase.

Her store had air-conditioning, one of a few in town. I needed a cool down. Dipping down the first aisle, I posed as a serious shopper. Whistling softly, I glanced over at some tiny cups and saucers. Mrs. Poodie spotted me instantly. She zigged and zagged like a Heisman contender down the china plate aisle waving her arms. Within seconds, she stood in front of me with her hands out.

"Jake, let me see your hands," she said, inspecting them carefully. She glanced back to the front of the shop, hoping I didn't spoil a big sale.

"Miss Carter, I have a new set of Spode China. Just arrived from overseas," she yelled, letting my hands drop to my side.

I wish I had a nickel for every time I heard Mrs. Poodie say that. She always said the same thing: "Just arrived from Germany, France, or some other faraway place." All you gotta do is turn one of those plates over, and it says, "Made in U.S.A."

"Mrs. Poodie, I washed my hands before I came in—promise." My hands were clean. Spotless, even. Momma often scolded me for spending too much time washing my hands. "You're gonna rub the hide right off, Jake," Momma would say. Mrs. Poodie straightened up and rolled her glued-on lashes. Her teeth moved up and down when she spoke, like they were all loose.

"You and your scoundrel buddies have dirty fingers, Jake Travis. I don't have time to continuously rid the entire shop of chocolate spots every time you choose to loiter around. Those hands haven't been washed in weeks. Didn't you see the sign on the front door? It specifically says, 'NO LOITERING.' I hung it there just for you and those other three brutes."

"What does that word mean?" I said, scratching my head, glancing over to the door.

"It means," she whispered, "that you and your friends are not to step foot inside this shop, unless you are looking to purchase something. Now scoot. I have paying customers." She placed her hand in the middle of my back and pushed me toward the front door, saying "Scoot." She hurried off to the front of the shop, muttering something about the new tulips just arrived from Holland. I'm not very smart, but I know that Legit, Texas, was not on the distribution list from Holland for anything, much less tulips.

I marched out of the shop, turned and read the sign taped prominently to the glass door, "NO LOITERING." Huh. I had sufficiently cooled off. Nothing in that store I wanted anyway. Standing on the sidewalk, I studied my hands and peered through the window once more before moving on. Finding my soup can, I started for the whittling bench, daydreaming about my abilities to kick fifty-yard field goals with one second remaining on the clock.

There is Jake Travis, lining up his kick. It's up…it's good!!!!

CHAPTER FIVE

Wisdom from the Bench

LEGIT, TEXAS, had three schools of higher learning: an elementary, a middle, and a high school, yet those places couldn't hold a candle to the education a kid could glean from the whittling bench. It was the origin of all rumors and a few truths. If it happened, the bench discussed it. If it didn't really happen, it soon would.

As I turned the corner from Main onto Laurel, there they sat. The long bench was cut from an oak tree. Its log legs set in concrete. The bench had no back but sat near the outside wall of Snedeker's Drugs and Dry. The men chewed God knows what, drank strong coffee, and whittled things only a kid could appreciate. This was my lucky day—no other boys lingered—hoping to cop a few coins for running errands. All three were in deep conversation and didn't notice my arrival.

"Yep, Sheriff Bevis said it hisself," Curley said, pacing in front of the bench, waving his arms. "Got a large one out in the back pasture. Seems like he sells the shine to the coloreds across the river." On most Saturdays, the bench attracted three local characters.

Curley Snedeker, who owned the drugstore, seemed to live on the bench. He sold everything from Band-Aids to shotguns—usually right from the bench. In Legit, he probably sold more hand guns than penicillin. A twitchy guy with a spare tire and sweaty forehead, he smiled continuously and enjoyed rubbing my head like I was plucked from a Lucky Charms box.

Known around town as temperamental hot heads, Curley and Buck Herndon went at it every day. While best friends, they argued over almost anything: politics, women, cars and manure. "I just can't believe it. He's a deacon at the church. How on earth does he sleep at night?" asked Buck.

Buck owned the local newspaper, the Legit Gleaner. He spoke with a loud voice that belied his skinny frame. He liked pouring whiskey into his coffee cup throughout the day. Considered the leader of the bench, Buck's healthy appetite for scandal resulted in starting most rumors. People in town often thought Buck would post a photo of his momma running naked down Main Street if it sold papers.

Sam Davis held the bench together, though. He was the ballast. He didn't have a job, other than whittling cool stuff. "Probably sleeps better than all of us together," said Sam. "He buys a new car every year. Not just a new car…but a Caddy. According to rumor over at the Man Shop, he's always buying a new tie and jacket. I heard from Maude over at the Chat & Chew that he has two pair of Stuart Mc-Guires—those babies ain't cheap. Nope, I don't think ole Limp has any problems sleeping. He may, on the other hand, have a problem staying awake. I hear he's moving shine between midnight and three in the morning."

"There ain't nothing in the Man Shop cheap," said Buck, rubbing at a red stain on his starched white shirt. "I paid ten dollars for this damn tie and got half of the Chat & Chew on it."

"I should talk to Bevis," said Curley. "He and I go way back…to the second grade." Curley believed that getting beat up by Sheriff

Bevis in the third grade gave him an inside track to police work. "I could get him to take a look at it. Could be a helluva story there, Buck. A front pager burner. Hell, you might even win one of them Grammys. Why don't you investigate the place? Hell, ain't that your job?"

"Investigate Limp Wiggins' moonshine still? What are you nuts, Curley?" Buck said. "That old man owns more guns than the South during the War. Nope. Don't want Doc Moore pulling number eight buck outta my ass, and besides my reporters are committed on more interesting human interest stories. And Curley, it's a Pulitzer not a Grammy, you ignorant ass."

"Who you calling an ignorant ass?" Curley jumped up and poked his finger in Buck's face. "Buck, your idea of a human interest story is Miss Lea's cocker spaniel having her litter of pups. Ain't got no people in it. How in the world can it be a human interest story?"

"What the hell do you know about nothing, Curley? I uncovered that marijuana garden last year, south of town. That was a front pager. And where did you learn to talk like that? 'Ain't got no.' Jesus, did you actually attend a school of higher learning, or did you buy that diploma from Texas A&M like your pappy did?" Buck's face turned red with the heat of debate.

"If I recall, Buck, your sweet daughter, Lucy, caught a bad case of the confessions. Tells you she's smoking weed and drives you over to the pot pasture. Hell, a fucking blind man could've broken that case. And you leave my family outta this, or I'll plant you on the pavement right now," Curly said, outraged now.

Curley took two steps back and assumed the fighting position, his fists raised tight. Buck struggled to get his feet under him but soon got it together. They stood toe to toe, each waiting for the other to throw the first swing.

"Did they teach you how to spell in that welding school?" Buck laughed. "They surely didn't teach you to speak English, you old goat." Buck and Curley faced off.

Sam stopped working his pine with a long blade, looked up, and said, "Hang on boys. You're not being a very good example here for our young friend."

Finally, Sam glanced down at where I stood and got up to separate the two old men. "Don't you have some drugs to sell, Curley?" Sam pushed Buck and Curley apart.

Curley turned and saw me lurking at the other end of the bench. "Oh. Yes, I do. Lots of sick folk around here with that twenty-four hour flu and all. The cold and flu season is gonna bite us in the ass— uh in the rear. See you guys later on over at the VFW?" He turned his head to meet mine. "Hi there, Jake. How's your daddy doin'?"

"He's over at Chester Jones's picking up some feed," I told Curley.

"Well, tell him and your momma howdy—see them at church to-morrow," Curley said as turned away.

"Yessir, Mr. Curley. I'll tell 'em."

Curley clapped his hands and made for the corner of the building. "Boys, see you later over at the hall, and Buck, you can kiss my ass you old fart. Bring your best poker-face tonight, 'cause I'm gonna clean you out. Gonna take your drawers, Buck. You wait and see. All your money, your drawers, and then I'm gonna kick your butt."

Buck sat back down on the bench and looked over at Sam. "He really pisses me off."

By this time, Sam had seated himself again and resumed whittling his pine. "He does have a way of provoking you, but if I recall, his read of the marijuana bust was spot on." Sam set aside his whittling. He reached down, pulled out a can of tobacco and papers, and be-gan to roll a cigarette neatly into a long, thin line. He liked to smoke King Albert from the can. I noticed Sam's long gritty fingernails as he lifted the roll to his lips.

"What's your point?" asked Buck, tugging at his collar and check-ing his powder blue leisure suit for stains.

"Sometimes he likes showing you the mirror, and sometimes you dislike the person staring back," Sam said.

"What're you ... some kind of head shrinker?" Buck waved the comments off and sipped his coffee.

Sam looked over at me. "What's your take on this, Jake?"

"Well, I dunno, Mr. Sam, but it seems to me that Mr. Curley might need some underwear and a rear-end to hold them up."

Sam smiled, parting the road maps of lines and wrinkles on his face. He shook my hand and patted me on the back. Sam's hands felt used and callused. I imagined the stories those hands might tell. "Sit down here, son. Glad you could come see us," Sam said.

I sat down next to him and kicked my can between my feet, watching him shave the piece of wood he held in his left hand. "How's school, Jake?" he asked, turning the wood over and over in his hands, holding it up to the light to get a better look.

"Real good there, Mr. Sam," I said. "You fellas got any errands you need done? I got a bit of time and could sure use the work."

"You're late, boy," Buck slurred, still pissed at Curley. "The Kline twins stopped here 'bout an hour ago. They're delivering the papers to Quincy's grocery—as we speak." Buck poured some whiskey from a tin into his coffee cup.

Of the three, Buck had the most opportunity for us kids to earn money since he owned the only newspaper in the county. A quarter a trip was standard fare. Buck liked to whine about his overhead, the cost of printing and ink. Like that stick in Sam's hand, Buck whittled us down to nothing. But Sam always slipped me a dime or nickel for a sweet candy run.

"Why don't you just sit here with us and whittle a bit, Jake? You haven't been here in a few weeks. It'd be nice to catch up."

"I didn't bring my knife with me, Sam." Momma was stubborn about these things. She would not let me have my own knife until I was of "age"—whatever that meant.

The old man reached deep into his coveralls. He plucked out a small buck knife and opened it for me. He offered me a small piece of pine wood. "It's real sharp, Jake—be careful," Sam said.

"What'cha working on there, Sam?"

"This piece of wood is called basswood. It's soft and is used in all kinds of musical instruments. I'm making a pan flute. See?" he said, showing me the long round piece of wood.

"Pan flute?" I scratched my head. "Do you play it?"

"Yep." Sam reached down into an old bag lying behind the bench. "Here take this one home and learn to play it."

I placed the flute in my mouth and blew hard.

"Here," Sam said, "put your fingers over the holes and don't blow so hard."

I blew it again. Softer. A clear, hollow note sounded.

"That is pretty neat, Mr. Sam. Thank you very much. Would you show me how to carve something like that some day?"

He nodded and said, "Sorry, we don't have errands for you today. Maybe…next week."

"Not your fault, Mr. Sam. I'm saving my money to buy a shotgun," I announced.

"You don't say," Sam said. We sat in silence for a few seconds. "Buck here says he has a job opening for a crack reporter."

Buck laughed and pulled out a shiny new quarter from his pocket—tossing it over to me.

"Thanks, Mr. Buck." I caught the coin in both hands, careful to not drop it. "I promise to put it in my piggy bank, for my gun."

Buck smiled. "Don't mention it, son. Come over to the store—I'll make you a good deal on a used Winchester. Just keep it between us bench boys. Okay?"

"Mr. Buck, I could do that reporter job."

"You think you could be an investigative reporter, do ya, Jake?" asked Buck, grinning wide to reveal teeth destined for a dental visit.

"I think I could. I'd have to ask Momma, but I could do that job. I mean, I still gotta go to school and all."

"Maybe someday when you are older," said Buck, standing to leave.

When you're older. Heard that over and over all my life—how do you know when you're older?

Buck tossed his cold coffee into the grass and rubbed his forehead with both hands to improve circulation. "Sam, I'll see you later at the poker, uh...meeting." He picked up his newspaper. "Jake, tell your momma and daddy hello for me. Maybe see you in church."

Buck turned the corner for his office, his gait uneven and wobbly from all of the coffee he drank.

After he left, Sam showed me how to whittle the wood without losing an appendage. We didn't talk a lot, but we sat on the bench soaking up the shade and the mild breeze blowing in from the north. I cut at my wood until it was sharp and then reached for the flute, studying the holes in the end.

"Sam," I started, "what kinda job you do? I ain't ever seen you anywhere around but on the bench."

"Well, Jake, I used to be in the Army." He bent over and showed me the scar on his forehead. "Got shot up in France, during the war. Still can't think straight sometimes. I had limb shakes and headaches for years...take a bunch of pills just be able to hold my knife steady."

"Were you scared in that war, Sam?" I wondered what it was like to be shot with a real gun.

"Sure, I was afraid every day I was there, Jake. German soldiers firing cannons over my head. My best friend, lying next to me in a fox hole, bleeding to death. I didn't think I was gonna make it out alive."

There was a long silence before he finally added, "I prayed really hard to get out of that fox hole in one piece, and the good Lord saw fit to get me out of that bind."

"Do you think Jesus listens to all prayers, Mr. Sam?" I asked.

"Yes he does—you just gotta keep sending them up. Be patient.

God doesn't always answer them in your time, you know."

"Do you think he answers all prayers?" I needed to know.

"Sure of it, Jake." Sam paused a second and slowly sat his knife on the bench. He looked down at me with his calm blue eyes. "Is there something you want to tell me? Want to talk about?"

"No sir," I said. Then added, "I just wondered if Jesus could make bad dreams go away. In Sunday School, Mr. Behannon said bad dreams are nothing more than movies of bad things we do."

"Well, the way I look at it, Jesus can do anything he sets his mind to. Don't give up on Him. Keep looking up, Jake. As for Mr. Behannon," Sam shook his head, "I wouldn't put too much stock in what that ole Bible thumper says. Ok?"

Sam sensed my confusion and patted my knee. He turned to me and said, "Son, keep looking up. That's where you'll find the answers to your questions, even the ones you are afraid to talk about."

"I'm not afraid to ask questions," I said.

"We're all afraid," Sam said. My eyes locked on the can between my feet, and I sensed his eyes searching my thoughts. "Jake, questions lead to answers, but many times, we're not ready to hear them spoken out loud. Have faith, young man. The answers will come when the time is right."

Sam waved and smiled to a lady down the street. "There's Miss Irma going into the Chat & Chew cafe. I'm gonna walk down and visit with the late lunch munchers. See you later, Jake, and think about what I said. Oh yeah, almost forgot—left you something under the bench. You'll have to look hard for it."

"Nice talking to you, Sam. See you next Saturday. I'll be here earlier for chores. Ok?"

Sam waved and disappeared across the street.

I crawled under the bench and looked around. There lay a silver dollar in the corner. I picked it up and turned it over and over. Shiny and large. Holding it in my hand reminded me of the time Dad let me hold a silver dollar last summer. The bad dream woke me up, and I cried out during the night. He walked quietly into my room and turned the lamp on. Lying down beside me, he hugged me tight. Dad believed my dream was about monsters. He explained that a silver dollar was the only thing monsters were afraid of. Shoving a silver dollar under my pillow, he kissed me goodnight and switched off the light. I fell asleep—coin held in my hand, praying the dream would not return.

I crawled back up on the bench and wondered if Sam knew what he was talking about. Just keep sending them up. Jesus could make bad dreams go away.

He was right about one thing. I was afraid to tell anyone . . . including Jesus.

CHAPTER SIX

My First Best Friend

ALL COUNTRY BOYS HAD CLUBS, and ours was a double secret club where death by hanging awaited any member with loose lips. The club had three members, and girls were not allowed to visit—anyone who suggested such would be tossed out and branded a traitor. The clubhouse was built near a stream, hidden deep in the thick piney woods, and provided ample cover from the German tanks that routinely traveled about the cleared pasture a few yards away.

The president of our club was Smitty Grinds. He was rather large for a third grader. Actually, Smitty was supposed to be in the fifth grade, but he said he wanted to stay behind so we could all be pals. We all thought that was pretty cool. Truth be known, Smitty just didn't have it all there. He would study and study, but for some reason, he couldn't master the classroom. With three older brothers, he sported a black eye about once a month, and the older kids in school called him names and teased his hand-me-down clothes. Smitty spent more time in the principal's office than the principal.

I first met Smitty in the second grade. Before the school year even started, I was chosen to be in Mrs. Ratcliff's class. My friends and I coordinated our requests for placement to the principal's office early and often through our moms. Mrs. Ratcliff was older than dirt, had a hearing device mounted on her head, and moved at the speed of a turtle. We would have it made, plus Momma loved her.

Cozy as a litter of baby opossums, we had our way in her class the first week. The day started with her reading all the names one by one from a typed page. It took forever to finish reading the roll call through her thick glasses lenses, and we did our part to stretch it out.

"Jane Anderson," she read, with her large round eyes squinting in search of Jane, who always sat in the desk up front. We traded seats during roll call and answered.

"Present. Over here. Over here, Mrs. Ratcliff," Jane said, waving her hand wildly.

"Thank you, Miss Anderson, dear."

"Mickey Baldwin…Mickey Baldwin."

"Not here," he yelled, sliding down into his desk.

"Very funny—Mr. Baldwin. For that little prank, young man, you get to put your nose in the circle of bad for the remainder of roll call." She pointed out the faint white circle scrawled on the board and demanded he stand facing it. He rose from his desk and mimicked the mummy walk to the corner. "Mickey, you might feel especially comfortable in the bad circle, as your father spent most of his second grade year standing where you do now. And, I might add, he spent two years standing in that spot."

"Yes'm, Mrs. Ratcliff." He placed his nose on the chalk board.

In Mrs. Ratcliff's class, our lives were as perfect as candy on a stick. Then one morning, Mr. Poodie, the principal, stepped into the classroom. He whispered something into Mrs. Ratcliff's ear, turned, and called my name.

"Jake Travis, will you come down and join me in my office?"

Who, me?

I thought I did something terribly wrong. Despite my tendencies for monkey business, I had never been called to the principal's office for any kind of big trouble. Walking the silent corridor behind Mr. Poodie, I reviewed all of the mischief I made during the first few days of school. Was it the red food coloring we poured in the front fountain? No way could he pin that on me. Was it the "fatty-fatty" sign we taped to Sharon Thomas' back? Of course not—plus she liked the attention. Maybe it was the fresh cow patty we hid by the library door. Nope, came up empty.

He ushered me into his office and asked me to sit in an oversized chair. Mr. Poodie's gray desk was large enough to land a plane and contained only a single, thick file and a yellow No. 2 pencil.

Mr. Poodie smiled at me and asked, "Jake, do you know why I asked you to come down?"

"Huh. No sir, Mr. Poodie. I ain't been in Mrs. Poodie's store in weeks though, and I didn't take that chocolate-covered cherry she had out on the table for her paying customers. It was Mike Pruett. I told him not to, but what can I do? He's in the fourth grade. Have you seen how big he is?"

He gently laid the pencil down, held up his large hands, and waved them in surrender. "Jake, I didn't call you down here to discuss my wife's flower shop or any other inappropriate behavior you might be guilty of. Although, I'm sure she'll keep an eye out for your friend Mike."

"Mr. Poodie, he's not my friend," I pleaded, as my voice cracked with emotion. The tears were mounting, and I felt the wet drip about to spill from my eyes.

"Jake, relax. Take a deep breath." He opened the manila file sitting before him. For a second grader, my file looked awfully thick.

"Jake, we're going to make some changes in class assignments. I realize that it's well into the first month, but Mrs. Ratcliff cannot handle more than twelve youngsters. Other teachers have only nine kids, so we've decided to move you into Miss Wade's class."

What? Hold on a minute. Who's this Miss Wade lady? I tried not to stare at Mr. Poodie's dangling nose hair as I considered this news.

"I'm terribly sorry to move you now," he said. "I feel for you, and know you're good friends with many of the students in Mrs. Ratcliff's class, but it's got to be done. I assure you that you'll be able to see all your friends at recess and lunch." Mr. Poodie looked at my pitiful tear streaked face and closed the file. My life is over, I thought.

"Miss Tate will escort you down to Miss Wade's class. Good luck, Jake." He plunged the file back into a drawer and whisked me down the hallway to where Miss Tate stood waiting for me.

That's it? Good luck?

"Yessir," I managed, wiping my face with my shirt sleeve.

Miss Tate smelled nice, and she helped me gather my books and supplies from Mrs. Ratcliff's class, holding my hand as we walked the long empty corridor over to the next classroom.

"I think you'll really like Miss Wade," Miss Tate comforted me. She's new here and is a very kind lady. She's lucky to get you in her class," Miss Tate said, removing her lace handkerchief and dabbing at the tears on my face. "Now, be brave, Jake."

When I entered the classroom, Miss Wade paused mid-sentence and placed her eraser down on the chalkboard. All eyes turned to me. I quickly scanned the room for a familiar face. A big kid sat in the third row looking like he needed a shave. Kristina Kline, the meanest girl in school, sat across the aisle from him. She smiled and licked her lips with her meaty arms crossed. Even boys in the upper grades were afraid of Kristina.

Not a friend in sight.

Miss Wade ambled over and held out her hand. "Hello, Jake. My name is Miss Wade. How are you?" I lifted my head to the ceiling, it seemed, before I met her eyes. Her bottle-thick glasses made her eyes appear larger than a fifty-cent piece. When she stooped to say hello, I noticed she had more teeth in her mouth then all of the men over on the whittling bench put together.

"Fine . . . I guess, Miss. Uh . . . " I muttered, head hanging down, fighting back the tug of tears.

"Wade. Miss Wade," she said. "My name is Miss Wade."

"Okay." I did not want to face the classroom.

She ushered me into the center of the classroom as Miss Tate said goodbye. I stood there holding my belongings tight to my chest, hoping she would not put me near Kristina.

"Well, just peachy," Miss Wade said. "You'll be sitting in the empty desk behind Smitty Grinds on the third row. Smitty, stand up so Jake will know who you are. Girls and boys, let's welcome Jake Travis to our class."

In unison, all of nine kids screamed, "Welcome, Jake Travis!"

I heard Kristina say something nasty under her breath, something about an arm and a socket.

"Okay. Kristina, let's be nice," Miss Wade said, shaking a bony finger at her. After the noise settled, Miss Wade ushered me down my row—like Daniel to the lion's den.

I lifted my head and strained to smile, eyes darting about. The kid who needed a shave stood and waved me over. He was a giant by any second-grade standards. I dipped and dodged my way between the desks, glancing at the faces staring up at me. Sitting down at my desk, I slid my things under the top and took another peek around. Kristina gave me the mean look, cocked her fist, and held it against her nose.

"You're dead meat, Jakey boy," she whispered, her arms bulging. I was pretty sure she could snap me in half while eating a peanut butter sandwich.

I listened to Miss Wade preach about addition and subtraction, but my head didn't follow it. Why me? Didn't they like me over in

Mrs. Ratcliff's class? I felt miserable, and to be honest, I was deathly afraid of Kristina. The last thing a guy needed on the playground was talk that he got beat up by a girl.

Within a few minutes, the bell rang. Recess at last. I hustled to be the first out the door, watching for Kristina. I walked over to the main steps of the school building and sat with my head in my hands. My life was indeed over.

"Jake, don't feel bad, man. I'll be your friend," I looked up and saw Smitty Grinds. He wore a big smile and kicked at dirt clods in front of me. I noticed his tennis shoes. Black high-tops. Cool. "And don't you worry about that witch Kristina. I told her if she messed with you, I'd snap her head off. You ever watch Andy Griffith?"

"Sure." I wiped a tear from my cheek. "All the time. It's the best show on the T.V. box, except maybe Bonanza."

"I like My Favorite Martian, too." he said. "Come on. You can be Barney, and I'll be Andy." Like that…we set off in a cloud of dust, and I never looked back.

CHAPTER SEVEN

The Double Secret Club

DEATH BY HANGING awaited any member of the Double Secret Club with loose lips. Smitty Grinds presided over our club. No girls allowed—anyone who suggested such would be tossed out and branded a traitor. Built near a stream, the clubhouse hid deep in the thick piney woods, and provided ample cover from the imaginary German tanks that routinely traveled about the cleared pasture a few yards away.

Hicker Nutt hollered out, "Do it doggie style baby," as he approached the clubhouse. Of course, none of us understood what this meant, but it became our club motto. Settling into the log cabin, Smitty opened the Double Secret Club meeting with the strike of his gavel.

"Order. Order," Smitty pounded a wooden gavel, borrowed from his uncle who was a retired judge from Roganville.

"Order, order!" He banged even harder.

"Dammit, Smitty, we're in order," our vice president, Hicker Nutt, said. "You're gonna break my table, and Momma'll kick my butt."

The square, white plastic table and four matching chairs, all borrowed from Mrs. Nutt's restaurant, sat in the center of our clubhouse, where we were clustered. Hicker urged Smitty on, demanding, "Get on with it, will ya. I gotta be home by dark."

"Okay, okay. Keep your shorts clean, Hicker. Our first order of business will be a report from our intelligence officer. Jake, you now have the floor," Smitty ordered.

Built from pine saplings and parts from a '55 Chevy Impala, the floor of our clubhouse consisted of plywood planks.

I provided intelligence. "The three of us have been busted by Mrs. Poodie and are branded loiterers," I reported. "She even taped a big sign on her front door saying so. She said it to my face. If she catches us in her shop, she's gonna call the Sheriff and have us thrown in jail." Their eyes went wide.

"So, what does that mean?" Smitty asked. "Loitering. You know she's from France. Could be a French word." Smitty launched a dart at the board hanging at the other end of the clubhouse...missing the board completely. "Crap. Your turn...Hicker."

"Nope," I said. "Not French. I checked it out with Sam, down on the bench. Sam says loitering is hanging around a store with no money."

Hicker laughed. He tossed a dart at the board we rescued from the dump and said, "Well, Sam ought to know—all that old goober does all day long is loiter."

"Heck, Jake, half the ladies who go in that store ain't got no money," Smitty said. "They call it shopping around." He threw another dart. "Bulls-eye, baby."

"You crossed the line, Smitty," I said. "That one doesn't count."

"Bullshit, worry wart." Smitty marched to the board, pulling out his dart.

"Jake's right, you were beyond the line," Hicker tossed another at the board. "That's cheating...you know."

"Okay. I was beyond the line," Smitty snapped, "You pecker-heads want to arm wrestle over it!" Hicker and I looked at each other and shook our heads.

"Nope, we both know how that turns out," I said. No matter how hard we tried, we never beat Smitty at darts…or arm wrestling.

"Jake's right about the old ladies," Hicker added, reaching for a grape Nehi from the old Coca-Cola cooler in the corner—another treasure found at the dump. "They go in there to eat the chocolates on her table and listen to her brag about her china cups."

"But they got something we don't have," I said, grabbing a root beer and popping the top.

"What's that?" Smitty asked.

"The look," I said. "Sure as rain, most of those ladies don't have any money to buy Mrs. Poodie's fancy plates and stuff, but they look like they got money. You see?" Both Smitty and Hicker nodded letting my words soak in, shaking their heads in dismay.

"She's got the best chocolates in town. I'm gonna miss sneaking in there," Hicker said.

"Me too," said Smitty, cocking his head. "But you know…it's kinda cool—sort of like having a 'wanted' poster in the Wild West. Hell, boys, we're famous. We shouldn't be griping about it. We ought to be celebrating. We're wanted!" Hicker and I looked at each other. "If we get thrown in jail by Sheriff Bevis, Momma's gonna tan my butt," I said, downing my root beer. "Boys … relax. Let's not over react. What else you got, Jake?" Smitty asked. I gave them the run down on what was happening over at the bench. I shared the conversation Buck and Curley were having about Limp Wiggins' moonshine still.

Hicker interrupted me, "What's moonshine?"

I speculated it was something illegal, and old man Wiggins was selling it to the black folks across the river.

Smitty sat there. "I know what moonshine is, Hicker. It's home-made booze. My granddaddy had a still before he became a judge."

Smitty's biological pedigree was long and varied, and many of his relatives spent long nights in county jails.

"Homemade booze?" I asked. "You sure 'bout that Smitty?"

"Positive," he said, shaking his head. "The question is what're we gonna do about it?"

"What do you mean? Do 'bout it?" Hicker asked, looking at me for support. Buck was being pressured to investigate this whole affair. I repeated the brief exchange between Buck and Curley. Smitty and Hicker took it in, their eyes widening to the size of saucers.

"That's it!" said Smitty, jumping out of his chair, knocking it to the floor. "We can crack this case, boys. We're gonna take pictures of the still and give 'em to Sheriff Bevis. We might even get a reward."

"A reward?" I asked. "What kind of reward?"

"Money, Jake, green backs, baby. Could be a hundred dollars, maybe even more. Plus, we'd be heroes. Hell, if we bust this thing, Mrs. Poodie'll have to let us in to eat her chocolates. They might even ask us to be in the Legit parade. Hey, we might even get a medal!" exclaimed Smitty.

"I never liked old man Wiggins. That guy gives me the creeps," Hicker said. "Ain't never seen a man with more grease in his hair."

"Curley said he's got lots of guns in the house. What happens if we get shot? We could get shot, you know," I protested.

"Jake, you worry way too much. Relax. Take your underwear outta your crack for just a second. Ok? We just got to outsmart him," Smitty said, standing and pacing the room. "Plus, I got shot with my brother's BB gun two years ago, and I lived." He lifted his shirt to show us one more time the faint scars left by a loose BB shot.

"How do we prove he has a moonshine maker?" I asked. "My daddy heard he had machine guns hidden in the barn. I don't know, Smitty. This sounds dangerous."

"It's called a still, Jake, not a moonshine maker." Smitty paused his pacing and faced us. "Forget about the machine guns, boys. He ain't gonna see us. We're going in under cover and taking a camera with us. Take a bunch of pictures. Run them down to Mr. Buck for development. Heroes, boys. That's all we gotta do. Heroes. Like Audie Murphy in To Hell and Back."

We took a vote—three to nothing—and extracted a spiral pad from the shelf and proceeded to map out the plan.

On Saturday, Hicker, Smitty, and I arrived at the clubhouse early in the morning, dressed for war. Most folks drive into town for supplies and such on Saturdays, and we figured old man Wiggins would be gone like everybody else. I reviewed our supplies. First-Aid kit. Check. Camera. Check. Compass. Check. Binoculars. Check. Our fastest tennis shoes. Check-Check. Log-rolls in case of capture…check!

With black shoe polish smeared about our faces and Army helmets strapped tight against our chins, we lined up single file and marched through the woods to Wiggins' place. When we reached the edge of the woods, Smitty and Hicker crawled under a tree and loaded their BB guns. It was my job to secure accurate and timely intelligence, so I left them arguing over whose gun was more powerful.

Old man Wiggins lived at the end of a narrow, sandy dirt road. The two-story white house, begging for a new coat of paint, stood out in the dark canopy of pines. His metal barn garage was hidden behind the old house nudging a chain link fence that housed his barking hounds. There were plenty of places for me to hide out along the road, waiting for his dash into Legit.

Standing dead still between two tall oak trees not ten feet from the road, I sweated like a farm animal.

I heard him before I saw him, the engine of Mr. Wiggin's black Cadillac growled through the rutty sand, kicking up dust. He cut the corner on two wheels and bounced onto the paved county road.

As soon as he disappeared, I darted across the road, eating bits of rock and dust. Diving under the barbed fence, I rolled into the pasture. Urging my high-tops into overdrive, I arrived at the end of the pasture, gasping for breath.

"Okay. He just hit the highway doing 90, not five minutes ago." I bent over to catch my breath.

"Way to go, Jake, let's synch our watches," Smitty said.

"Wait a minute, Smitty; I don't have a watch," Hicker said. "You didn't say nothing 'bout watches."

"Me neither," I added, looking down at my bare wrist.

"Well, then. I guess my watch will be the one we keep time with," Smitty said.

Hicker and I stood staring at each other. "Smitty, the way I figure, we got one hour tops," I said. "Let's move it, 'cause I'm a little worried."

"You're right," Smitty said. "Who's got the camera? Hicker, that was on your list."

"Got it right here in my bag." He reached inside the large canvas bag.

"Let's take a look," Smitty said. Hicker pulled out a square black box with a crank on the side.

"Geez, Hicker, couldn't you find something older? This thing could've been used in World War II," Smitty said.

"It was my granddaddy's. Pop keeps it hidden in the barn. I've seen him taking it out a few times, usually on Saturday nights when he goes honky-tonking across the river. I ain't never used it, but it must work 'cause he takes with him every time." He pulled out a long black cord. "Look at this," he said. Smitty and I watched as he plugged it into the side of the camera. "All you do is mash this button, and it takes a picture." Hicker demonstrated for us. "See, we can take our own picture."

"Great idea, Hicker," Smitty said. "Okay, let's stand over here by the tree. Stand tall, boys. Look mean. This will be on the front page of the Gleaner, for sure."

Click. Heroes.

"Jake, you take point. I'll bring up the rear. Keep your eyes open and your mouths shut." Smitty liked giving orders. "If you see something suspicious, raise your right hand—like this." He demonstrated the movement a couple of times.

"Which hand is the right hand?" Hicker asked.

"Jeeeeeesusss Christ, Hicker, I ain't never seen a bigger dumbass," Smitty said.

Removing my black shoe polish from my bag, I placed a dab on my finger and rubbed it on his right hand. "There you go," I said, shaking my head at Smitty to let it go.

We decided to use the Bob-Tail Quail Call if we got separated. If captured, however, we were to scream at the top of our lungs. The Bob-Tail was one of our club's secret calls, and Hicker kept practicing it, which put Smitty in a tizzy. "Would you stop that?" Smitty demanded. "You are driving me nuts. I'm trying to lead us into battle, and you're back there playing with your fist."

"Cool it, boys," I said. "Keep it down." I kept looking around for a good escape route just in case old man Wiggins decided to cut his trip into Legit short. From what I gathered at the bench, this moonshine still was located at the rear of his pasture, buried deep amongst the large pines, brush and thorn briars. A dim road appeared before us. It weaved and disappeared, soon becoming a small trail. We swallowed hard and started marching down it.

"Lookie here," said Smitty kneeling to the soft ground like a scout on the open range. "Quite a bit of traffic back here. Tractor tires all right." Smitty was boastful of his ability to read any kind of track. Horse, cow, deer, or raccoon. He knew them all. That was one of the reasons we made him president.

Hicker glanced over and gave me a nod. I, on the other hand, was as nervous as a tick on a hot skillet. I've always had an alarm that warned me when things were not good. It was ringing loud and clear.

"Maybe we should turn back," I said, looking behind us.

Hicker and Smitty looked at me. "What'cha talking about, Jake?" Smitty asked. "What are you . . . a sissy? Stop worrying. Heck, we're almost there." Smitty turned and gave us the right hand motion to move out. I turned one last time and stared down the narrow trail. Nothing.

Ten minutes later we dropped behind the thick bushes. The old, cut log barn was open on the sides with an enclosed room in the center. Smoke drifted from a pipe on the roof. There was a red Ferguson tractor sitting beneath the overhang, with stacked hay bales lining the rear. A single door was centered on the front. After Smitty gave us the down sign, we dropped to our bellies and crawled, blackberry briars ripping at our faces and arms.

I first noticed the silence. It was like all the animals in the forest escaped to hide from the sins of this man. The enormity of the trees blocked all light from the area, giving it a look of early evening. The hair on my neck tingled. I reached into my pocket and felt the silver dollar, resting there. Protecting me.

I also noticed the "KEEP OUT" sign hanging on the front door of the barn that read, "TRESPASSERS WILL BE SHOT." Holy smokes!

"Smitty," I whispered. "You see the sign on the door?"

"Shush, Jake. You worry too much," Smitty said, crawling faster.

"Well, somebody better."

We commando crawled through the briar patch and leaned against the side of the barn, sweat dripping down our faces. There were no windows, and the door was secured with a large pad lock. It looked like we were screwed. "What're we gonna do?" I asked. "Looks like Mr. Wiggins has this placed locked up tight. Guess we'd best get going, huh?"

Hicker's orange hair and freckled face nodded so slightly. He'd had enough, too. I could hear my knees shaking as we sat there pulling stickers out of our arms.

"Hicker, go around back and see if there's a window or back door or something," Smitty said. Hicker hesitated a second and then bolted around the corner. Smitty inspected the lock like a professional. I watched the trail, my heart beating through my shirt. In a few seconds, Smitty slid back down beside me.

"Tighter than my granddaddy's wallet," Smitty said. "The only thing we can do is blast it open. Boy, I wish we had a grenade or some dynamite."

I looked at him. "Got an old Blackcat firecracker in my knapsack," I said, taking a look inside the bag.

"Not enough. That there lock is too big," Smitty said.

About that time, Hicker crawled back, eyes wide. "I got a way in. Come on." A potato cellar in the rear of Wiggin's barn lay open. Bingo, no lock. We scrambled to the old cellar and stuck our heads into the hole. Smitty looked at both of us. "Hicker, you go first."

Hicker looked into the pit of blackness and asked, "Why, me, Smitty? You're the president. You ought to be first."

"You found it, Hicker—I want you to get the credit," Smitty said, staring into what appeared to be a bottomless pit. Smitty was tough as nails during daylight, but deep inside, I think he was afraid of the dark. His momma and daddy fought a lot and most of that happened deep into the night. I knew how he felt.

"Okay," Hicker said, turning and lowering himself down the steep ladder. We all followed close behind, and when our feet touched the dirt floor, we stood as still as church mice. It smelled of kerosene. I wished I hadn't watched that Dracula movie last weekend. Where was my garlic when I needed it? We were standing so close together, I was not sure if it were my knees knocking or Smitty's.

"What'dya think might live down here?" whispered Hicker. "You thinking a ghost might be down here?"

Ghost? Thanks a lot, Hicker.

No one spoke for a few moments, as we stood toe to toe in the darkness. "We need some light. Who's got candles?" Smitty finally asked. I pulled a box of kitchen matches from my sack, struck one, and held it as high as I could. A long slender bench divided the square room. Mason jars filled with clear liquid lined the walls. Dry hay covered the dirt floor.

When the flame sputtered out, I lit another match, touched the wick of the candle, and sat the candle on the bench. The room came to life. "Wow. That's shine, boys. Lots of it," Smitty said, bouncing to the shelves along the wall.

"What're we gonna do?" I said. "Should we take some to Sheriff Bevis for evidence?"

"We need to taste it first to make sure," Smitty said. "We ain't gonna take a jar without knowing if it's shine or not." Smitty took a jar from the shelf, opened it and smelled the contents. "Smells like shine." He took a sip. "Tastes like shine."

"How do you know what shine tastes like?" I asked, dipping my nose into the jar.

"Look, Jake, I know for sure it ain't water. Take a shot," Smitty said, handing me the jar of shine.

I took a sip. "Yuck. That tastes like my grandma's flu medicine," I said, giving it to Hicker, who took a big gulp and shook his head.

"Whew! That's strong." Hicker said.

"My daddy says real moonshine can cause blindness, and if you drink too much, it'll make your pecker fall right off," Smitty pronounced, gesturing to his crotch. Hicker and I glanced down and stood there wondering how our lives would be different. Smitty offered up another shot, and Hicker and I both shook our heads. Best be cautious.

The moment was shattered by a noise above us. We froze. "Did you hear that?" Hicker whispered, moving closer to me.

Smitty placed his finger against his lips. "Shush."

We tiptoed side by side to the ladder and peered up into the bright opening. Nothing. I slid over to the bench and fetched my sack. Boom. Boom.

"Holy shit. Was that a gun?" Hicker squealed, trying to blow the quail call into his fist.

We scrambled through the room, knocking over shelving and the bench. Jars crashed to the dirt floor. The candle flipped off onto the dry hay, and flames erupted. I stomped the blaze with my shoes, but the flames were faster than my feet. Smitty clutched an old blanket, but the blaze grabbed hold, and he quickly tossed it aside. The heat grew intense, and within seconds, smoke filled the room. Breathing was hard.

Boom. Boom.

"Let's get out here—now!" I said. "Hicker, forget the quail call. Run for your life!"

We scrambled up the ladder, pushing and shoving to the opening. Once clear, we ran without looking back, deep into the woods, dodging tree stumps and briars. There was an explosion. We skidded to a stop, huffing and puffing. The flames reached for the tree tops. Dropping to our knees, we sat there in silence for what seemed an eternity. Our bodies shook uncontrollably. Within a few minutes, we heard a siren blaring in the distance. I looked around for my sack. It was nowhere to be seen. Hicker had tears in his eyes.

I turned to Hicker and whispered, "Where's the camera?"

He stared at the flames and pointed at the barn. "I don't know."

What had we done?

CHAPTER EIGHT

Session One

(2004)

THE DOOR PLATE READ MEL ALLEN, PHD.

I had never undergone therapy, but had been known to play the role of a psychiatrist on long, boring airplane trips.

I cracked open the door to the office and stepped inside a small empty waiting room. A miniature, round table separated two leather chairs. No plants. The art on the wall reminded me of a Holiday Inn, stark with the class of a mobile home park leasing office. I glanced around and cleared my throat like it would announce my arrival.

Maybe my sly doctor had some hidden cameras watching my every move. Hell, if I were seeing nuts every day, I'd have an armed guard standing by. No cameras that I could spot, although, the painting of President Washington looked a bit suspicious. I stood up and stared into his eyes, wondering if a hidden television looked back.

I'm a prompt guy. Always have been. It's in my nature to arrive almost everywhere early. Maybe that does not make me prompt but really premature. Huh. I thought about that for a second. Not sure I want to go there with the ole head shrinker. I think it goes back to my very first official date in high school. I told Tess Starks I would pick her up at 7 p.m. I arrived at her house early, thinking we might make the drag before the movie. I was about to ring the bell when she opened the door. There was shock on her red face.

"Hi, Jake. What're you doing here?" she asked, her eyes telling a story that only the two of us knew.

I assumed that one, she had forgotten about our date; or two, she had found a bigger fish during the last twenty-four hours. Both were not good. I struggled to think of a number three, but my mind turned to the large guy standing beside her. I recognized him by the Neanderthal spacing in his teeth. Eger Deets, but most people just called him Moose. He drove a Chevy truck, fitted with large rim tires and loud chrome pipes. The flames along the side panel said it all. The entire school knew when Moose drove into the parking lot. Another sign of his arrival was the scattering of small guys, like doves in a corn field. Eger loved pounding on freshmen.

"Well, huh. You know. I was driving by and wondered if you had completed Mrs. Krouse's Chemistry assignment." That was lame at best, but considering the large guy with his arm around her neck was the starting linebacker for the ZeDonk varsity football team, I felt like a ballerina with no shoes.

Tess was a nice girl. She had confided in me that she and Eger were on the outs and that she needed a fresh start. See the town through a different windshield was the way she put it. She was also bright. She caught my "Hail Mary" pass with a slight wink and took it in for a touchdown.

"Gosh. That old hag gives us more homework than any of our

other teachers combined. No, I haven't, but as soon as I do, I'll give you a call. Maybe we could meet over at the library tomorrow afternoon. We could share our notes and answers." She glanced at her watch. "Why don't we say 2:00?"

"Sure. That sounds great." I back-pedaled at a fast clip toward my ride. Tess broke Eger's grip on her shoulder, descended the stairs, and hopped into the Chevy, glancing back at me over her shoulder. Embarrassed.

Just as I was about to open my car door, Eger's shadow blocked the afternoon sun. I'm not sure what he ate as a child, but I imagine it was mostly his siblings.

"Hey, Travis," he growled, holding the door to my ride.

I cleared my throat. "Yes, Eger."

"You played a great game last night. Watched you real good. Keep it up—you might find yourself blocking me during varsity during practice."

Just what I always wanted. My head handed to me every afternoon at football practice.

Nevertheless, Moose let me live to see another day. So, I liked being early—it saved my ass countless times.

The opening of the door brought me back to the waiting room and George Washington. A young lady, early thirties, looked over at me with what appeared to be pity, then disappeared without even a hello. Frail as a bean pole, she wore something made from a hemp plant. She had been crying.

Wow, I thought. This guy must be brutal. I'm not sure I wanted to go through with this. Maybe there was another way. My palms were damp, and I wiped them repeatedly on my slacks. I glanced at the clock on the wall. One o'clock on the money.

The door to the inner office opened, and an older, yet attractive woman with long, gray hair pulled back into a bun stepped through the doorway into the waiting area.

"Are you Mr. Travis?" she asked, smiling. She looked like she had just stepped out of Woodstock.

"Yes. I'm Jake. Uh, Travis. Yes, that's me."

She stood still in the doorway. If she grabbed a guitar, she could be Janis Joplin.

"I'm sorry," I said. "I arrived a bit early and have an appointment to see Dr. Allen. I was just looking around. Nice place you have here, especially that painting of George Washington." Trying to be funny, I smiled and cracked, "Did Dr. Allen personally know the first President?"

Her pale, blue eyes looked sideways at me through wire rimmed glasses. "Of course...you're Jake Travis, and my book says you do have an appointment. Why don't you step inside, make yourself comfortable. Dr. Allen will be with you in a moment." She disappeared through the door into the hallway.

I stepped inside and surveyed the place, which was furnished like a comfortable living room. Certificates and degrees littered the walls. Some photos of places and people sat atop various tables and the desk.

I wiped my sweaty palms on my pants. I didn't want this guy to think I was suffering a nervous breakdown, but to be honest, at this point, a dozer couldn't pull a straight pin out of my ass.

A few moments later the door opened.

"Hello, my name is Dr. Allen," she said with a slight grin, walking toward me, her small hand extended from an orange sweater.

I guess the look on my face said it all.

"I'm sorry," I stumbled. "I thought you were his secretary out there. I was expecting..."

"Ah—a chimpanzee, perhaps?" she interrupted. "Not to worry. My abbreviated name gets me that reaction a lot. Actually, I enjoy the shock on my male patients' faces when they find out that I am a grown woman. It reminds me of the natural social discrimination that men have in our society against women."

Oh my God. A bra burner. Just what I needed.

She paused as I surveyed the photos hanging on the wall. "I hope that's not going be a problem—my being a woman."

"Uh, of course not," I stuttered. My arm pits felt drenched. "It's a little confusing, you know."

"So, do you suggest I place a disclaimer on my business card?" she asked, smiling at my anguish. "I'm going to pour a cup of English breakfast tea. Would you care to have some?" She reached for the steaming pot and arranged her tea bag in the chipped white china.

"No thanks, maybe later." I watched her as she stepped through her ritual. Tea bag, hot steaming water, milk, and one cube of sugar. The corner gas fireplace looked unused as did the overstuffed chair positioned in the corner. It was piled high with books. The leather couch looked cracked and worn. "Where do I sit? Couch okay?"

"Yes, of course," she said, taking a seat directly across from me. She blew on her tea and sat it down on the wooden coffee table separating us.

I liked her casual sophistication immediately, yet felt frightened of her at the same time.

"Why don't we get started?" She opened her notebook and held a blue BIC pen in her left hand like a NASCAR driver gripping the wheel. "Why don't you start by telling me why you came to visit me?"

"I'm sorry, but I'm not sure how to do this," I said, twisting in the leather chair. An expensive Indian rug covered the oak floors of the room. I searched for guidance. Found little help.

"I have found it best during initial visits to just get to know one another a bit. There are no hard and fast rules here. Let's just take it a step at a time. For instance, like, where did you grow up?" Dr. Allen asked.

"In a small town—Legit."

"I've heard of it. East Texas…right?" She paused. "Actually, a tiny place, isn't it? I think maybe I've driven through it, going to New Orleans." She reached for her hot cup of tea and sipped.

"Yes, we like to refer to Legit as simply—quaint." I uncrossed and crossed my legs trying to find a comfortable zone.

"Are your parents living?" she asked.

"Yes, both Mom and Dad still live on the farm, where I grew up. It's not a big place, but it's home." I explained.

"Tell me about your relationship with your parents."

"Well, I love my mom and dad. I mean, I'm not here because I hate my parents or anything like that. They were, are, great parents. Of course, we didn't always agree growing up, but they worked hard to provide for all of us. Dad worked the farm and at the plant. Mom stayed home, worked, and raised the three of us. I felt loved growing up." I paused. "We had tough times making ends meet, but I believe they did the best they could. All things considered, I feel blessed."

Dr. Allen tucked her legs underneath her as she relaxed in the overstuffed chair. She never stopped taking notes. The look she gave me started me again.

"Neither Mom nor Dad went to college. They were married short-ly after graduating from high school. Actually, I found out, not too long ago, that I was a mistake. Mom was pregnant with me when she and Dad were married."

"How did that make you feel?" Her eyes examined me, surveying my body language.

I held up my hand to signal a pause. "Excuse me, should I call you Dr. Allen, Dr. Mel Allen, or simply Doc?" I was buying time.

"What would make you feel comfortable?" She rested her pen.

"Personally, I would like for you to call me Jake, not Mr. Travis, and I would prefer to call you Mel."

She reached over the space and gripped my hand. "Jake, pleasure to meet you. I'm Mel. Now, how did it make you feel being in the dark about all of this for apparently, a very long time?"

Time's up.

"I felt cheated, I guess. I mean, they stayed married all these years, and they never thought to tell me. Maybe they were embarrassed. During their day, it wasn't a good thing to be pregnant out of wedlock, I'm sure. I suspect there was a lot of pressure on both of them. I admire them for sticking it out. But, to be honest, I felt sad that maybe their lives would have taken another path, had it been different."

"Do you mean, would they have made different choices had they not had you to consider?" she asked.

I sat there thinking about how she put that. I guess we all have choices that are driven by circumstances that are out of our control. "Something like that."

"Have you asked them if they have any regrets?" she said.

I looked to the Indian rug again. "No, I let it go. What's to be gained from making them relive something that happened so many years ago? Something maybe even painful for them."

She looked at me and closed her notebook. At that specific moment, I did not realize the impact of the words I'd just spoken on the rest of my life. She sat her notebook and pen on the coffee table.

"Do you think their telling you would have made a difference in your life?"

"I guess I would have liked to have known."

She reached her notebook but stopped. She looked up at me, "I sense the notebook is a distraction. Today, let's just chat, get to know each other. Okay?"

I took a deep breath and began again. "I know Mom and Dad tried hard. It was more difficult for me, money wise, than for my brother or sister. While they were not light years behind me, they were just enough younger so that the money situation was better."

"Did you feel cheated somehow that they had it easier, so to speak?" Mel asked.

"No…not at all. I was actually grateful they had it easier."

"Let's talk about your siblings. Start with your brother."

"He is four years younger, and my sister is six years younger."

"They both live here in the city?" she asked, pulling the loose hair from her face and tucking it behind her ear. Mel wore little or no make-up, but she didn't need it. Her face was long, narrow and fresh. She wore a beige, cotton dress, and the sweater had been violated by a family of moths. Feet clod in plaid socks and Birkenstocks, she likely voted the liberal ticket.

"Yes, they do," I responded.

"If I ask you to give me one word that describes your relationship with your brother—what would that be?"

I cleared my throat. Something lifted into my throat. I swallowed hard.

"I'm not sure I totally understand the question."

She cocked her head. "Jake, you're very bright, and you're buying time with these little venues. Spit it out. This is not some type of test here. I want you to be spontaneous with your answers. The first thing that comes to mind."

"Responsible would be the word, I guess." I wondered what she saw on my face.

"As the oldest, being responsible was a big deal, particularly growing up." She paused. "Why did you feel responsible for your brother?"

"I think it goes back to when we were pretty little. He and I were walking home one afternoon, and an older kid in the neighborhood pushed him down on the asphalt. His knees were banged up and bleeding. I took him home and watched as Mom and Dad washed him in the tub. He cried and cried, and I felt horrible. My dad scolded me, saying that it was my job to watch over my little brother. From that day forward I watched over him. I tried to protect him from bullies, even when I was the one leaving with a black eye," I said.

"Do you still feel responsible for him today?"

"I do. I know that seems weird, but for some reason I still do."

"What bullies do you have to fight off today?" she asked.

"Well, I am not sure where to start with that. There are lots of bullies. I mean, he's my little brother, and I would never want something to hurt him. Sometimes I feel like he needs my help," I explained.

"These bullies you talk about; how are they trying to hurt him, and why do you need to protect him? He's not much younger than you—right?"

I was not sure where to start, but decided to let go and see where it leads. At this moment, there were many things I needed to say to her. She was giving me courage, and I could feel her energy pushing me to open up. It was horrifying, but at the same time, I felt something good may wait for me on the other side.

"My brother seems to be gay," I said, wiping my hands on the leg of my pants.

"Seems to be?" she asked. "Is it possible that he may not be?"

"No, I mean—no, he's gay."

"And you feel responsible for his homosexuality?"

"Well, I'm thinking maybe it was my fault."

"How could something like that be your fault?" she asked.

"Well, bad things happen in families all the time, Mel, and I'm concerned maybe it happened to him, as well." The last two words were almost a whisper. Maybe she didn't catch the meaning. I was praying she didn't. There are some secrets that should remain buried. There are some sins we never stop paying for. Those are the ones that wake me in a sweat and demand my guilt.

"Bad things? Can you be more specific?" she asked.

"Abuse."

"By bad things, are you suggesting he may have been abused by someone in your family?"

"Yes, that's what I am suggesting."

Mel said, "Children who suffer abuse or trauma don't have a higher tendency for homosexuality than the rest of us," she said. "I can understand how you might fear something dreadful could have happened, causing his homosexuality, but that is not the reason someone is gay. He is gay. There are lots of theories behind that, but in my opinion, people are born that way."

She paused her thought. "All these years, you have felt responsible for your brother's sexuality because of suspected abuse?"

"Because maybe I should have said something to someone," I said, staring at the lines in the Indian rug.

"Did you see something inappropriate happen to your brother when he was young?"

"No, I didn't."

"Did he ever say something bad happened to him?"

I shook my head no.

"How long has he been gay?"

"I'm not sure, but I guess for a long time. I denied it for a long time. In my family, if you don't talk about it, it really doesn't exist."

For some time, she and I talked about what I knew, how I became aware of it, and whether or not he actually told me. My little brother sensed I was living in denial, and he finally told me straight out to put me out of my misery. I created all kinds of scenarios. None of them true. Even when he spoke the words to me, I tried to deny them.

After a bit of silence, she looked at me and said, "You are concerned that your brother is gay. You are struggling to understand how to deal with that, but at the same time, you have a sense of responsibility for his sexuality. Is that because you feel responsible, as his brother, or that you knew something and failed to speak out?"

She was digging in a grave of skeletons.

"Look, Mel, what should I do? He's my little brother. Maybe I can get him some help," I offered.

"Help?" she asked. "Are you convinced your brother needs help or could it actually be you who needs help?"

We let those words simmer in the room, neither wanting to touch them. Guilt and shame wrapped me like an ice-cold blanket. I had never told anyone. Maybe speaking about it would have made a difference in his life or perhaps, even mine.

"Jake, your brother is gay. He does not have a rare or incurable disease. His sexuality is neither your responsibility nor your fault." She paused and chose a pillow to rest her arm on. "Do you love your brother?"

"Of course, I love my brother. I'm not sure I understand the question," I said.

"You have absolutely no power over someone's sex life, and the feeling of responsibility lies in possibly other things. If you love your brother, why not just simply accept and love him for who he is?"

I hesitated. "You mean to ignore this, uh, lifestyle? A lifestyle that I don't even understand or condone?"

"What makes you think he understands your lifestyle?" She paused, "Jake, let me put it this way. You have two basic choices. Accept him or deny who he is, and he will eventually disappear from your life. At that point, you will no longer feel responsible for him, thereby letting you off the hook."

"Wait a minute," I said, "you think this is all about me? I came here to figure out how to continue a relationship with my brother, who informs me that he is gay, and you are telling me all I want is off the responsibility wagon?" I didn't want to leave this room like the poor lady before me. I wasn't going to cry in front of this woman, but I was a nanosecond from just that.

Mel argued, "If you love him, love him. You have to love all of him, though, and to be honest, you might find if you let go of the social static, it might not be near as scary as you believe. And for the record, this is all about you, Jake—not your brother and his sexuality."

I let out a deep sigh and retreated somewhere deep inside. I wasn't certain of how much time had elapsed since we began, but my body felt like I had been running for miles. In essence, I had been running for most of my life. Before arriving, I pictured myself leaving this room with a checklist of some sort, a set of rules by which to deal or understand. None of that made sense to me now. I was ashamed of myself for feeling what led me here. I loved my brother. Always have. What was I so scared of?

Mel looked at me and sipped her cold tea. "I think we've made some progress. Do you?"

I simply nodded in agreement.

Mel began to wrap up our session. "I realize our time is almost up, but Jake, I must ask you one last question if that's okay with you. If need be, we can go over our time, as my next appointment cancelled earlier today."

"Sure," I said, feeling the urge to vomit on my shoes.

She moved to the edge of her chair and watched me like she could see my every flaw etched across my forehead. "Will you tell me what happened to you?"

I wasn't exactly sure when the tears began to drain down my face, but I do remember it was a well that was cold and deep, and it demanded to see light. I nodded my head no. That was not something I was prepared to talk about.

What was she doing? That was a secret stored away, and I wasn't to speak of it. When I could no longer hold back, I slid from the couch to my knees, my head in my hands. When she reached over and placed her hand on my shoulder, I felt relief, and the well poured from me until I was empty.

CHAPTER NINE

The Truth

(1984)

ALMOST TWO DECADES PASSED in the blink of an eye, and our moonshine still secret remained among Smitty, Hicker and me. Not even our wives knew about it. It was the kind of secret if spoken out loud, you'd fear your life would end.

Our tenth high school reunion arrived before I knew it. The event, as in years past, was held at ZeDonk High. Some teachers attended. Most kids from our class returned. Those absent, were somehow not missed. Punch and cookies were served with heavy doses of stories, some factual—most outright lies. A few former students brought their children and a few brought spouses. The yearbook was once again passed around the crowd for signatures and finger pointing.

It's funny what a decade does to a bunch of youngsters. Some guys with long hair in school were balding and others had carpet glued to

their skulls. The biggest surprise was Kristina Kline, now an adver-
tising executive living in New York—smart, witty, gorgeous, and a
champion kick-boxer. She had a lot of practice growing up.

The only people at the reunion who hadn't changed much were
the three of us. Smitty, Hicker, and I met up at the party. Something
happens when you graduate and head off into your own world. We
swore an oath we'd stay in touch like brothers, but time flies when
not watching. We exchanged bear-hugs and high fives. Our pokes
and jokes eased the tension among us, and soon we were nine years
old again, flying through the piney woods and open pastures, searching for enemy tanks.

Smitty Grinds graduated and got a job in the chemical business, selling explosives to the construction industry. It was right up his alley. He
could sell better than most, and it seemed appropriate he would end
up in a line of business involving both bullshit and blasting.

Hicker Nutt bought the Legit Gleaner from Buck Herndon and
made it successful. His editor's column, "Cracking the Nutt," was
popular with the locals. I'm a subscriber, and it takes a full week for
news of the little town to reach me on the road.

We agreed to meet up at the clubhouse later in the afternoon.
Hicker gave the two of us a gritty smile and said he had a surprise
for us. "Don't be late," he commanded as he climbed into his pickup
truck and waved goodbye. Smitty and I exchanged family updates
and decided to mingle with the hot girls from school before leaving.

Most of us stood around the offices, where many times we'd been
called for spankings. A desk phone rang in the corner. I ignored it for
a few seconds, but after several more rings, I decided to answer it.

"Hello."

"Hello," the deep voice said. "This is Mr. Joe Folk, the principal,
aka G.I. Joe, could you please step into my office, Jake Travis? I need
to paddle your ass."

"Who is this?"

Just then, old classmates spilled out of the back room, laughing and congratulating each other on the ruse. I slid over and high-fived each of them. We caught up on all important things—fishing spots, hunting stands, and the latest Star Wars picture.

The small crowd of ex-students was beginning to move outside, so I waved goodbye to the boys, as we promised to go fishing someday.

When done, I weaved through the office desks lining the walls, stopping to lift an ancient receiver from the cradle. The phones must be thirty years old, if not older. Holding the receiver in my hand reminded me of the weary days I sat near the phone after the Wiggins fire. Staring down at the receiver, I remembered waiting for the Sheriff to call my momma and daddy, telling them the bad news and then dragging me off to jail.

The Wiggins fire set off a lot of rumors in Legit nineteen years ago. I remember the whittling bench was wild with speculation about what happened that day. White folks believed the black folks were responsible. The black folks were secretly delighted Wiggins got his due. Oddly, Wiggins remained silent and disappeared from Legit not long after—never spotted again.

The Gleaner ran a front pager about the barn catching fire. Nothing was ever printed about the gallons of moonshine that exploded and almost burned up the south end of the county. Curley and Buck had their own theories. Buck was convinced it was a still malfunction. He seemed to be an expert in moonshine stills. Curley figured Wiggins torched the place for the insurance money, and he seemed to know all about how that was done.

I always suspected Sam knew exactly what happened, and if he did, he carried it to his grave. He and Sheriff Bevis were childhood close, and I figured he was in the know on what actually went down. Since that day, I spent countless hours sitting on that old bench, and Sam never spoke of it. When asked about it, he would shrug it off and change the subject. Sam died a year after the fire. They found him propped up against the whittling bench, clenching his knife and pine.

Something inside of me died that day. Every kid needs a friend like Sam to set out the truth no matter the hurt. "Keep sending them up, Jake."

None of us dreamed the Wiggins fire would lead to a secret bigger than Legit.

"Don't be late." I remembered Hicker yelling before he left the re-union hall. There was something about how he said it, though. Like it might be important.

The dirt road leading to the back pasture is now poorly paved and lined with dented mobile homes, used tires, and washers. Loose bloodhounds chased my truck down to the pasture gate, running 'til their legs gave out. Slowing to a stop, I noticed that Smitty and Hicker had beaten me to the clubhouse.

I announced my approach using the "Do it Doggie Style" song. From a few yards away, I heard them join in. The clubhouse was near ruins, but considering we had not been back since our ZeDonk graduation night, it looked pretty good.

Ducking through the small door frame, I saw dated Playboys scattered on the floor, with aged pin-ups tacked against the wall. Even Samantha Stephens was still up there. A few grades ahead of us in high school, she landed the inside bunny spread. Her Playboy fame lasted about as long as it took the ink to dry, and then she was gone—never heard from again.

Smitty and Hicker crouched around the plastic table—bucket of cold beer sitting between them. Hicker held a large manila folder tucked under his left arm like he was protecting the Queen's Shield. His right hand held a large joint. He lit up as I stepped in.

"Hey guys, how'd you beat me?" I smelled the weed as Hicker blew smoke into the air.

"Grab a beer. Take a seat. Take a hit. Really…good stuff," Smitty said. Pointing at Hicker, he continued. "Hicker's got something he wants to tell us."

"What's the deal, Hick?" I asked, reaching for the joint.

He shook his head and handed me the joint. "Take a hit on this ... you're gonna need it."

I obliged him with a deep inhale. Smitty had apparently indulged before my arrival as he was giggling like a twelve-year-old girl at a slumber party.

Hicker told us to shut up and listen. He recounted the entire affair from the very beginning.

Sheriff Bevis retired this year. He had been sheriff in Legit for twenty years and served as the town barber for almost thirty, both jobs running concurrently. When we were kids, we would line up outside the jailhouse for our summer cut. Getting your hair cut from a guy with a .38 Special strapped to his hip was about the coolest thing ever. We would push, shove, and trade marbles to be first in line, and getting a good look at the latest bank robber in lock up was a big deal. Oddly, we never saw anyone in the jail...ever.

Of course, Sheriff Bevis gave only one cut and owned one razor, and he didn't take more than three minutes per kid. The good news was he charged only fifty cents, and we were good for the entire summer. I don't know if he was a good Sheriff or not, but he was a horrible barber.

Hicker was planning a special front page feature on the Sheriff to celebrate his retirement, so he stopped by the jail for an interview. He looked at both of us and started to recount his visit, leaving nothing to conjecture.

ॐ∞ॐ

"Come in, son," Sheriff said. "Take a seat over there." Pointing to a clean stool, he looked around at the boxes neatly stacked, ready for loading into his truck. "Excuse the mess. Been up here all week trying to get things sorted out for the new man."

"I guess after thirty years, Sheriff, you can accumulate a lot of memories," Hicker said, glancing around at boxes stuffed with photo frames, pistols and old fashioned hair clippers.

He chuckled. "You know what? It's odd really to even say this, but my fondest memories are from cutting all of you kids' hair. I watched you grow up. Watched some walk off to war." He lowered his head. "Cried when some didn't come home."

He paused a second to gather his bearings. The Sheriff had lost his only son in Vietnam.

"I truly don't have many good sheriffing memories to share with you, Hick. Legit's small time crime. Few thefts. Some marijuana patches. Occasional fist fight over at the auction barn. But generally, it was a good job. Never even fired my weapon in the line of duty. It did go off accidently one time. Scared the shit outta me." He paused. "I would prefer you not print that part about the gun going off, though."

Hicker nodded. "Of course not," he said, resting his pen on his lap.

Hicker sat back and listened to him. In some way, Bevis needed this time.

"Yep, not sure what's gonna happen to me now that the Mayor has decided to put me out to pasture. Likely fish more, worry less," Bevis said.

They continued to talk about specific milestones regarding the county. Its growth and how that impacted the type of crime committed in the area. With the Sheriff running out of things to say, Hicker gathered his pad, stuffed it into his backpack, and prepared to leave.

"Sheriff Bevis, we all thank you for a great job of taking care of us. I know when we were younger, we put you to the test many times. I want to thank you personally for all you did."

Raising his hand, he said, "Hicker, can you wait here for a moment? I have something for you...if I can find the damn box."

He disappeared into the back storage room, and Hicker could hear him opening and closing file cabinets.

After several minutes, the Sheriff returned with an open box. He plopped it down on top of a large wooden table.

"Hicker, I been meaning to give this to you for some time now, but just never did. It wasn't calculated, you see, but I wanted time to let things blow over. Understand?"

Hicker nodded his head, but said, "Uh, no Sheriff—guess I really don't understand."

"You 'member that moonshine fire over at Limp's?" he asked, letting loose a sly smile.

A week did not go by without Hicker thinking about that day. "Well, Sheriff, I think I know what you're talking about. It was a long time ago. Wasn't it?"

"The box is for you, Hicker. I'm sure you'll find the rightful owners of its contents."

A large knot rose in Hicker's throat, and trying to swallow was not an easy task. He was afraid to move, like he was plugged into a lie detection device that would send alerts out if he blinked even an eye.

"Son, take a look inside."

Peering over the edge of the box, Hicker's eyes grew wide. Inside the box were three items: a pair of old army binoculars, a writing pad with scribbles on the front, and a camera.

"Look Hick, I ain't never talked to no one about the evidence I found, scattered from the old barn to your clubhouse, which by the way, was never really a secret. You three boys beat it outta there so fast, you left an entire path of incriminating material. I followed it all the way to your clubhouse."

"Sheriff, I'm not sure what to say." Hicker cleared his throat.

Sheriff waved him off. "No need to say anything. I'm sure what you find in that box and in this file will answer a lot questions you, Smitty, and Jake might have," he said, holding up a manila file.

"But Sheriff, you knew all these years?"

"Of course I did. I might be a simple small town sheriff, but I'm a long county road from stupid."

Hicker was silenced by the man's words. After a few seconds, he said, "Sheriff, I'm really sorry we didn't come forward and speak to you about this."

"No need. Since that day, you three boys were models of Christian behavior. All three have turned out to be taxpaying citizens. Churchgoers. What more could I've accomplished by making your sins public or speaking with your daddies or even tossing your asses in jail?"

He continued. "All I ask is that you sit down, share it with the others and destroy all of it. Will you promise me that, Hicker? Promise an old man that you will not write one word about what happened then and what I did?"

Hicker stared into the tired Sheriff's eyes. "I promise."

∂∽∾

When Hicker stopped talking, I felt the knot in my throat and my heart beating against my chest. I remembered this feeling as a young kid. The night I walked into the living room to tell Mom and Dad about the dreams. Walking down the short hallway from my room took all my courage. By the time I arrived at my dad's armchair at the end of the house, it was gone. That was the last time I tried to gather the strength to share—the nightmares.

"Are you telling me Bevis gave you all of the evidence he found from the still fire?" I asked, grabbing the joint from Hicker and taking a deep and much needed hit.

"Yep," he said, grinning at both of us, "he knew the whole time."

Smitty was trying to soak up Hicker's story with another hit on the joint. At first, he looked dazed and confused. "You gotta be shitting me, Hicker. Is this some kind of set up?" He pointed at me. "There is no statute of limitations on federal offenses, you know."

"Sit down, Smitty. Relax." Hicker opened the box and stopped without removing anything. "Guys, this is surreal. I never thought we'd find out why things turned so upside down in Legit. It's all in this box."

"You've looked inside?" I asked.

"Yeah, this was months ago. I needed a good night's sleep."

Smitty and I nodded. We could buy that.

Hicker reached in the box and pulled out a faded writing pad. On the front was my name. Inside, on the first page, was my list of things to do and bring for the mission. There were simple maps showing the location of the still, the small road leading to the rear of the pasture, even the cage for his barking dogs.

I was speechless.

Next he reached in and pulled out binoculars. "I think these belong to you, Smit," Hicker said.

"Well, I'll be damned," Smitty said, shaking his head. "I got quite a licking from Pop for losing those. I could never tell him where I really lost them—so I made up some bogus story about losing them over by the lake. To this day, I can still see him walking after chores around the lake, head down, looking for these binoculars."

He paused.

"I never had the balls to tell him what really happened to them. Not long after, we were burying him," Smitty said, a crack in his voice.

Hicker and I glanced at each other and lowered our heads. Back then, most dads were pretty hard on their sons. They really knew no other way to be. Smitty's dad was harder than most—yet he loved him.

Hicker's eyes grew wide, reached in, and pulled out the black camera.

"Holy shit!" Smitty and I yelled in unison. "Holy shit!"

"Boys, you recognize this? Remember, it belonged to Dad, and I found it out in the barn. Seems he didn't really just keep it there, he hid it there."

"What?" I asked, trying to read Hicker.

"Dad hid this camera in the barn. Always thought he just kept it there."

"What? Why?" I asked.

"I wonder if we can have the film developed," Smitty asked, turning the black box around in his hands.

"No need," Hicker said.

"Holy crap, man." Smitty was reaching for the folder now held in Hicker's hand. He dodged Smitty's reach.

"Yep, boys. Bevis developed the film all right, but he did it in Beaumont, so no one in Legit would ever know."

Hicker opened the file. The first photo was the three of us, standing in the woods, dressed in army fatigues, black shoe polish smeared on our faces. We each held a Ranger BB gun and wore a broad smile pasted on our faces.

Heroes.

"I made copies for you guys. I thought you might like a souvenir." Hicker passed out the photos.

"What else is in the file?" I asked. "You're holding it like it's full of gold."

"Boys, reach down between your legs and grab your scrotum, 'cause what I'm about to show you will blow your mind," Hicker said.

Opening the file, I could feel my armpits dampening and my heart rate dropping to a level of an emergency room physician yelling, "Clear!"

"Behold boys—the real reason Sheriff Bevis never discussed this crime with anyone."

There were several photos lying on the table. I snatched up a single sheet, trying to make out the faces. Grabbing for another, I recognized two people smiling at the camera. One was Hicker's dad and the other was Mrs. Poodie.

Legit's a small town, and most townsfolk know each other. I was not expecting a simple black and white photo of Mr. Nutt and Mrs. Poodie standing in front of an old barn.

Hicker beamed. "Take a look at this one."

If I had awakened with my head stapled to a two-by-four, I wouldn't have been more surprised. The photo was wrinkled and faded, but there was no mistaking the two smiling faces. Mrs. Poodie was on the left, wearing nothing but a pair of cowboy boots, panties, and a lace bra. She held a fifth of Jack, and from the smile on her face, she and Mr. Nutt had consumed most of it before the photo.

There were ten photos in all. Each bared a little less clothing and a lot more whiskey smile.

These pictures answered decades of questions. Why did Mr. Poodie suddenly take another position in a school a hundred miles from Legit? Why did Sheriff Bevis never call? Why did Mrs. Poodie become real nice to us?

We were stumped. "Who took the photos?" I asked.

Hicker smiled. "Who was the Sheriff's best friend? Every time he talked, he reminded us how he saved Bevis's ass back in Korea. How they grew up together."

I looked at Smitty. We collapsed over laughing, holding our sides, remembering those moments from the bench. Oh, God no. Not him!

"Curley Snedeker!" We screamed out, falling out of our chairs.

CHAPTER TEN

Back Seat Driver

(1972)

MY FIRST CAR WAS A HAND-ME-DOWN. It was a long, white, four-door 1968 Chevy Impala, pre-owned by my parents. The ride had bad wheel alignment, flimsy shocks, and no power steering. In short, it was like driving an aircraft carrier down the road—I had to pay attention.

I kept the rims shined and the cloth interior spotless. The radiator coil leaked like a sieve every time I took a right turn, so most of routes involved left turns only. Not cool to arrive at a date's house smelling of antifreeze.

The seat cushions were black and littered with holes where springs eased their way out. Most of them were on the passenger side, forcing the girls to sit a bit closer. Oddly, my buds saw the genius that I was and pulled the same trick.

The car radio worked only if parked beneath a power line, so I saved my coins and purchased an eight-track tape player and fitted it with cheap home speakers that were bitchy loud. At that time in my life, loud was pretty much all that counted. There was no feeling like making the drag with Steppenwolf at full volume.

Shuggie Coleman, widely known around town as Gigolo, initiated my driving test. Although no one ever called him Gigolo to his face, he got the nickname for bedding most of the cheerleaders in school. Legend has it—all at one time. No shortage of miracles in East Texas.

Still, the test was the test. I remember how my entire body was covered in perspiration, even my feet. The test required a parallel parking move. Keep in mind, the only parallel parking spot in my hometown sat in front of the courthouse and was reserved for Sheriff Bevis.

Gigolo apparently had his eye on my cousin. He must have asked me to introduce them a hundred times in the thirty minutes of the test. Of course, I caught the hint way early and worked it hard. We spent half the test parked in the courthouse parking lot talking about my cousin. I passed my driving test. Never had to parallel park. Hell, I barely had to start the car.

The first week after being endowed a piece of plastic with my photo on it, I decided to maneuver the old gal to the Neches River, near the border between Texas and Louisiana. There was a place called the Pelican Club that would serve anyone with greenbacks. Hell, the underage crowd kept the place solvent.

I met some friends there on Saturday night. We drank quarts of Pear beer, which tasted a bit like bad urine. But it was beer, and we were having a high time.

After a few, I decided to point the Chevy home. It was approaching midnight, and my curfew was hauling me back to reality. As I bobbed and weaved the two lanes, I intentionally stayed off the main road, hoping to avoid any run-in with the local police department.

Going to jail is not something that looks good on a résumé, although many in Legit seem to think it was a badge of courage.

I floored the Chevy over the major highway onto my dirt road, and the coast was clear as the night. I gave a sigh of relief and kicked her up a notch. Didn't need to blow through curfew the first week. I have plenty of time to accomplish that feat.

Suddenly, out of nowhere, lights broke the darkness in my rear-view mirror. Red and blue and blinking. I slowed to a stop, dust kicking up in the headlamps.

All I heard was a tap on the window. I eased it down.

There stood Sheriff Bevis, a long flashlight in his hand and a frown on his face. He took the light and shined it in my eyes. I'm sure they were glassy and bloodshot. I was dead meat.

"Jake, you're in a hurry," he said. "You got some kind of emergency?"

"Yessir, running a little behind on my curfew."

"I wouldn't classify that as a true emergency, young man. Would you mind stepping out of the car?" he asked, backing a few steps to give me room. I tried to hold my breath, knowing it smelled of bad beer and borrowed cigarettes. Both could land me in jail.

"Where you been?"

"Oh, just around. You know. Around."

Wow. That was inspiring, but I figured the less said, the better.

The old sheriff let out a grunt. "Around? Did you just happen to go around the Pelican tonight?"

Busted.

"Uh, I might've driven by there. Curious, is all. But, I didn't stop. I can tell you that, Sheriff."

"Really, now? Did you happen to notice the white sedan with the little lights attached to the top?" He pointed back at his car. "It says Sheriff's Department on the side. Big letters. See?"

A new word flashed through my tiny brain. Stupidshit.

"No sir. I didn't see you parked there. I arrived at 8:00 and left twenty minutes ago. I had three beers, smoked some cigs, and ate a hot dog with cheese chips."

He smiled. "I didn't say I was parked there, Jake. I simply asked if you saw it parked there. I've been home all night overdosing on Marge's baked stew and watching the Aggies get their asses kicked," he said.

Thank God I didn't confess to tossing that skunk in the city pool. I was really close. This guy was too clever for a mere sixteen-year-old.

I lowered my head, knowing it was time to lick the dog's ass.

My knees were shaking, and the beer was barking for an escape. One didn't help the other.

I stood as straight as my body would allow. He smiled. "Okay, you're a good kid, Jake. I don't want to ever catch you drinking and driving again. Understand? Now, I want you to get back in your car and drive home. I'm going to follow you all the way to your house. If you screw up at any time, I intend to wake your daddy up."

"Yes sir, Sheriff, sir. I really appreciate it," I said, stammering like a kid reading poetry.

I reached over, opened the car door and crawled in, pulling the door shut behind me. I could still see him standing outside the window, watching my every move. There was a lot of pressure, and my bladder was screaming louder as I searched for the ignition key and steering wheel. They were gone. As a matter of fact, the entire dash board had vanished while I stood outside.

I closed my eyes and clenched my jaw. One Mississippi, two Mississippi.

There was a knock on the window, and I grabbed the knob and rolled it down a few inches. "Yes sir, Sherriff."

He cleared his throat. "Son, you might want to move to the front seat of the vehicle. I've found it to be safer and actually easier to drive from that position."

CHAPTER ELEVEN

Session Two

DR. MEL SAT ACROSS FROM ME sipping jasmine tea. It smelled wonderful. Her legs were tucked neatly beneath her, as she clutched the black spiral notebook in her lap. I wondered about the book and what it might reveal about all the hurts and secrets felt by so many.

There were some things left unsaid in our previous meeting, and I wondered where our discussions might lead today.

"So," she began, "I realize it's been a few weeks since our talk. To be honest, Jake, I'm surprised by your call. I doubted you would return for therapy, but I'm so glad you did. How have you been?"

"Good. Been on the road a couple of days. Nice to be home, though," I replied.

"Do you travel a lot for your work?" Mel inquired.

"On average, I travel a week or two out of the month," I said. "I've been doing that for a long time, and used to it, I guess. I enjoy the work. Travel can be a hassle, though." I sat on the soft couch crossing my legs like a girl with a dress too short for the party. Mel gave me a smile.

"How does your wife feel about all of this travel?"

I looked down at my hands. "She would like for me to be home more, I guess, but it is what it is."

"Does that put stress on your marriage?"

"We have two children, so it is tough on her, I know." I said.

"How old are the kids?"

I looked at Mel and smiled. "Our son, Griffin, is six and our daughter, Chelsea, is three."

She smiled back in that warm, comforting way. After a brief pause, Mel resumed. "Our last time ended with my question. I know it was a difficult question, and maybe I should've been more delicate in asking it. But...I sensed you needed to hear that question." She paused. "Did you think about it?"

"Yes, I did, and sorry about the emotion. I wasn't expecting all of this to be about me."

She smiled. "I wish I had a quarter every time I heard that line."

"I bet you hear all kinds of stuff," I said. "None of us really think we need to do this, therapy, I mean. I guess it's a shock when we find out maybe we do." I tucked my damp hands beneath my thighs.

"Have you told anyone about what happened?" she asked. "Your parents? Your wife, maybe?"

"No, I've never spoken to anyone about what happened to me," I said, standing up and moving to the teapot. "Do you mind if I have a cup of tea?"

"But of course. Help yourself." Mel sipped hers and gently returned her cup to the table. "Not even to your wife?"

"Especially...not to Joan." I removed the jasmine and tossed the bag into my hot cup. "I never said a word to my parents, either. Guess I was too scared."

"Why not say something, at least to your wife?"

"I was afraid you might ask that." I nodded, looking over to the potted orchid sitting on the window sill as I made my way back to the couch. "Not sure why. I'm good at burying things deep and moving on. I suppose I wasn't sure how she would react. Afraid she would think I was damaged."

I sat back down, staring into my cup at the steamy water turning darker as the aroma lifted.

"How long have you been married?" Mel asked.

"Twenty years."

"You were married right out of college?"

"Actually, our senior year in college."

"Where did you meet?"

"First grade. Joan and I grew up together," I said.

"Wow, that's unusual. So, you've known her most of your life?"

"Yes. We were friends growing up. We dated off and on during school, but mostly just good friends."

"Does she work?" she asked.

I shook my head. "No. When we graduated, she worked for a while, but once Griffin was born, we decided that she would work at home," I said. "I'm glad she did. She's a great mom. Our kids are incredible, and I think she was the reason."

"How are things at home? Do you get along?" she asked, standing and walking to the teapot for a fresh bag and water.

"Sometimes. I mean, we love each other, and while not every day is happy, we have good days and bad days. We muddle through both, with equal enthusiasm," I said. "Mostly, it's about the kids."

"When you have an argument, what's it about?" she asked.

"Oh, I don't know. Normal stuff." I paused to consider it more. "Kids. Money. Work. I seem to be a bit of a clean nut. I'm not sure why, but stuff scattered across the house bothers me—toys or clothes. So, when I come home, I tend to be critical of how things look. I wish it didn't bother me, but it does. That will usually start an argument, which leads to other things, other arguments. It soon becomes a vicious circle that seems to have no end. At night, we crash in exhaustion, and we start again the next day, with nasty words still hanging in the room."

Mel waited.

"I don't mean to imply that we argue all the time. There are days we don't say mean things to each other, for sure," I said. "We grew up friends. Sometimes, I wonder if we still are, though."

"Do you think you might be able to speak to her about this now?"

"No, I don't think so. Not yet, anyway. I'm in a weird zone at the moment."

"Ok. Fair enough. We'll come back to that later," she said. "How do you sleep?"

"Do you mean like which side of the bed?" I smiled, sipping my cup and wincing at the burn on my lips.

She laughed. "No, Jake. I am curious if you sleep well, or do you have dreams, and what those might be?"

"Sure, I dream. To be honest, though, I don't recall many of them."

"Did you ever have a dream that was recurring?"

My knees went numb, and my foot began to tap against the edge of the couch. "Maybe, a long time ago."

"Well, do you feel like sharing it with me?"

"Okay." I crossed my legs again, searching for the time on my watch.

CHAPTER TWELVE

Building Character

(1974)

"GOD DAMMIT, MALONE," Coach Jenkins yelled, blowing his whistle and throwing his towel to the ground. "If the corner comes up to take the back, you have to stay in and block. How many times do I have to tell you? Now, give me two laps. If I find you walking, you'll run 'til the sun comes up!"

The team watched Billy Malone start his laps. His head was down, sweat had soaked his jersey. He was a large boy, and I feared he might not make two steps. We'd been out in the heat since 7:00 in the morning. It was summer twice-a-day practices, day four. We were exhausted and sore. Water was passed out by coaches like it was an elixir of eternal life, seldom and only at breaks. Their goal was to get us to vomit. They loved it when we would toss our breakfast. I refused to give them that.

My high school football coach reminded me of an angry bull-dog—tall, meaty with a pocked-marked face that rarely tolerated a smile. A retired Marine drill sergeant, he was as mean as he was ugly. His goal in life was to make his players just like him. I had known Coach all of my life. I knew there was a large heart beneath the rugged stance, but he often left it at home during practices.

Our team was called the Mighty ZeDonks, and we finished high in the state playoffs last year. We were 10-0 and beat our opponents by an average score of 21. We had no mercy, as mercy was not something taught on our grass field.

The ZeDonk is a cross between a zebra and a donkey. Our opponents enjoy poking fun of our mascot, calling us the Jackasses or the inbred group from deep East Texas. Their tune changed when we took the field. Football was serious or not at all.

"Travis, get in there," Coach Jenkins yelled, kicking at a poor freshman player trying to get out of his way. I strapped my helmet on and ran to the huddle.

The quarterback began the call: "Twenty-four dive, right split, on two."

We ran to the line of scrimmage. There is no walking anywhere during practice. If you walk, you run laps. I got into my stance and watched as the corner began to sneak to the line. There was a blitz call on defense, and my job was to stay in the backfield and protect the quarterback. I bit down hard on my mouthpiece and gripped my fist.

"Hike!"

The cornerback paused a split second as the play was developing, then broke the line of scrimmage at a full sprint. His eyes were locked on my quarterback. I moved right and engaged a double block on the tackle, then released and came in high on the cornerback, putting my weight and speed into the hit. "Crack." We both landed in a bowl of dust.

"Holy shit," yelled Coach Jenkins. "That's what I'm talking about girls!

Helluva hit! Way to stay in there, Travis." He slapped my helmet with his hand as I walked to the huddle, but before I got there, he reached down for his whistle and blew it. Practice was over. There is a God.

The team assembled in the middle of the field. Coach stood in the center. We placed our hands on top of each others. "One, two, three. ZEDONKS. ZEDONKS. ZEDONKS." The huddle broke.

I walked over to the water cooler and collapsed. Dehydrated, I propped my feet on the bench, and watched as the team headed to the field house.

"Jake, you okay?" Coach Jenkins asked, standing at attention, hands on hips. He spit something dark onto the grass field and waited for me.

"Yeah, just a little tired."

Oh no. I placed my hands over my face. I can't believe I said those words.

"Really, tired are ya?" He smiled and blew his whistle, and the team stopped dead in their tracks. "Jake says he's tired. Get your asses back out here. Two laps for Jake. Come on. Let's move it. NOW!"

I started to get up and run. "Not you, Jake. You're too tired. Why don't you sit here and watch your teammates give you two laps."

I never spoke those words again.

Dad usually met me after practice. Sometimes he would ride with me, sit in the stands, and watch. On this day, he had pulled an all-nighter at the plant and had come directly to the practice field to watch. I showered, changed, and walked out of the field house. There he was, sitting in the car, asleep. He rarely missed a game or a practice. Sometimes he would leave for work after the evening practice and pick me up after practice, the next morning. I felt blessed.

I walked to the car and tapped his shoulder. "Dad, go on home. I'm staying here to watch the band practice. Catch a ride with someone later."

He sat up straight in the car seat, wiping his face. "Okay. If you need Mom to come get you, just call. I need you home by 2:00, though. Lots of chores."

"Will do," I said.

I tossed my shoulder pads and uniform through the back car window as he backed out of the parking spot. "Ask Mom to wash my uniform. I don't think I can wear it again. Pretty stinky."

He gave me a salute goodbye.

Most teens' social events were connected to either football or band. I was into both. Girls liked football players, but they played in the band. I figured I could double down. Reaching the practice field, I crawled up and sat down in the bleachers.

While our football team was always in the state playoffs, our marching band was equally as good. It won all kinds of ribbons and awards for music and marching. I played a decent trumpet. It wasn't because I had extraordinary talent; I had an extraordinary band director. Playing an instrument was not that difficult for me. Marching, on the other hand, seemed to stretch my capabilities.

As the band stepped through their marching routine in the blazing heat, I sat under a large pine shade and watched, recollecting the first and only time I had to march in the ZeDonk marching band.

It was my freshman year. 1971. Our school had hired a new band director from a college not far away. The story was, he had roots in Legit, but I'm thinking he must've pissed someone off up the ladder to be shipped back to this tiny spot on the map. His job was to turn around this ragtag team of musical misfits. Dr. Karl Wadenphful took the job seriously.

With his German heritage came a relentless search for perfection. First of all, most of our band members couldn't read a sheet of music if their lives depended on it. Secondly, we were kids, and most of us were in band because none of us wanted to take shop as an elective. Who in their right mind wanted to spend an hour a day with people missing most of their fingers?

Dr. Karl was on the tall side of short. His suits were cut and his shoes spit-polished. With his slack jaws, smiling required extra effort—energy he rarely spent. He had a lot in common with Coach Jenkins. One carried a whistle and one a baton. Both liked to kick ass. One did it with obvious intent. The other made you want to crawl through a keyhole to escape his wrath.

"People," Dr. Karl said, "this is the first ball game. Our first chance to show our parents and fans the Mighty ZeDonk marching band. If you can't memorize your music, don't show up. There will be no music carried on the field. Understood? As a matter of fact, if you can't memorize these three short songs before Friday, turn in your horn as you leave today."

I cleared my throat and raised my sweaty hand. "Sir, uh, Dr. Karl, sir?"

"Yes, Jack. What is it?" He lifted his hand in the air to silence the band hall. The room hushed.

"Well, uh, Jake, sir. My name is Jake."

"Jack, are you interrupting this band class to simply tell me your name?" he asked. "I know your name."

It really didn't matter. Jake. Jack. One letter is all.

"Well, sir, I am scheduled to play on the varsity team on Friday night. You have me listed on the marching orders. Just wondering if that was a mistake."

"A mistake?" He slammed his baton onto the easel. Pieces of it bounced into the flute section. "Are you suggesting that I make mistakes, Jack?"

The room was dead still.

"No sir."

"Good. I don't make mistakes, Jack. I've made my position clear with your coach. As a freshman, you're required to march. Those are the rules. I don't care if you are a star plucked from the heavens above. You'll be marching Friday night."

"But, sir, I haven't practiced with the marching band…yet."

"Then you have twenty-four hours to get ready. I strongly suggest you do just that. Now, if it's okay with you, we'll resume our practice."

When I said I played a decent trumpet, I was stretching the truth a bit. I was awful and failing to practice didn't help. This was nothing more than a power play between Coach and Dr. Karl. He didn't need me to march or play—he knew I sucked. As the new guy in town, he wanted to show he was in charge. Doc knew that sixteen football players would need to get carried off on stretchers for me to have a remote chance of playing. I felt like a cute girl stuck between two brawlers.

Since that afternoon, I had not slept much. I studied my marching position and talked to my section leader until I was completely confused. I dressed in my football uniform for the first quarter and a half. No injuries to report. I was cleaning the bench with my rear end. Midway into the second quarter, I rushed to the field house and changed into my marching band gear, hustling back to the stands as the band was preparing to take the field.

I found my position behind Wayne Bucher. He promised to not let me get lost. "Just follow the leader. That's all you gotta do, Jake." Sounded pretty simple.

We played the "Mighty ZeDonk" song as we took the field. Playing football was natural for me. You hit, tackle, and run. Marching, on the other hand, was completely foreign. My lips were dry as Grandpa's scalp and getting a buzz out of them was next to impossible. I made it to the fifty-yard line with no problem. The next routine was when time stopped for me.

I walked five yards, took a right. Walked another five yards and took a left. "Follow the leader, Jake. Just follow the leader."

My leader disappeared somewhere around the thirty-five-yard line. Vanished into thin air. Not sure if I was to turn or continue straight, but decided to continue straight. After a second or two, one of the twirlers walked in front of me. "Just follow the leader." Got it.

I turned and high stepped in behind her. By this time, I was gaining some confidence. I was playing, well, blowing my horn. I noticed she gave me a wicked look as I followed her to the twenty-five-yard line. I took it to mean stay close, Jake. "Follow the leader." She stopped and tossed her baton high into the air. I stopped with her and marched in place, all while playing as loudly as I could.

She marched right. I marched right. She marched left. I marched left. "Follow the leader." This ain't that hard. A monkey could do this, I thought.

"Jake, stop following me. Jesus, what are you doing? Are you nuts?" she said, tossing the baton high into the air. "You are supposed to be at the other end of the field. You're ruining everything."

Oh crap. I glanced down at the other thirty-yard line. She was right. The entire band was doing circles and shit at the other end of the field. I noticed most people in the stands were not watching them but me, including Dr. Karl who was running full speed down the sideline, waving his baton and yelling something at me. I could see his mouth moving but couldn't make out any words. I think I recognized a couple of curse words, but couldn't be certain.

To get my bearings, I marched in place for a second. Think quickly. This was bad. Real bad. I was the only band member at this end of the field.

Fuck it.

I marched as straight as I could toward the end zone, trumpet held high. I didn't rush it, lifting my knees with the tempo. I played my horn as I crossed the goal line. With a hard left turn, I marched to the other sideline, made another left turn, and strolled up the sideline. Making a sharp right, I marched up into the stands and sat down. The visiting crowd erupted into applause.

Dr. Karl didn't speak to me for a very long time after that. He also never asked me to march again.

CHAPTER THIRTEEN

Session Ten

THE RAIN POURED DOWN IN SHEETS. Unprepared for the downfall, I was soaked through by the time I reached Mel's office. She opened the door and noticed the puddle of water at my feet.

"Sorry. Thought I would beat the weather here. Obviously, I didn't." I dripped.

"No worries," she said. "I'm used to you being early." She glanced at her watch. "Wow. You're on time and on the edge of being late. What happened? You got a fever?"

"It was the street flooding down off of Central, under the overpass. Otherwise, I would have been here promptly—early."

"How about a towel? But stay out there," she yelled back at me. "That rug was handmade by some child in Turkey."

"A towel would be nice," I said. "Don't want to ruin your rug. I'll stay out."

"I'm kidding, Jake. I think I paid $200 for it at some tent along the highway. Come in. Take your shoes off. I could hear you squishing all the way down the hallway."

Mel disappeared for a second and returned with a hand towel. I stood in the doorway drying off. She just stood there watching me. I glanced down at her feet. She wore her wild socks. She was beautiful, and I shook my head to clear the thought. "Better. Thanks so much." I passed the towel. "What happened to your Birks?"

Laughing, she ushered me to the couch, offering me a new brand of tea. I watched as she darted and bounced from one end of the room to the other, arranging the soaked shoes, gathering her notebook, and removing the newspapers from the couch. I hadn't seen her like this before. She was a bit clumsy but in an elegant sort of way.

"Got caught in the rain, too," she said. "I had an umbrella, but found a deep hole in the parking lot. My shoes are soaked. They're sitting on the vent drying out. Here, give me yours, and maybe they'll dry out before we're done."

"Thanks," I said.

"I apologize," Mel explained, "Not usually this scattered. Had a doctor's appointment earlier and didn't have time to get prepared."

"Are you okay?" I asked.

She glanced up at me, as she sat down across and lifted her teacup. "Yes, I'm fine." Her eyes never left mine. She smiled.

For some reason, I didn't believe her. Mel immediately began asking questions. "Jake, what about fears? Do you have fears?"

"Well, I have many fears, a list too long to review in one session, for sure," I said.

She smiled and stirred a sugar in her tea.

"Seriously," she said, "I would like to know what they are. Give me two fears. Examples."

"Well, I'm deathly afraid of the dentist. Growing up in Legit, we had only one dentist. He had only one chair, owned a large needle and enjoyed drilling. What more can I say? We drank well water from early on, and maybe I was not as diligent in the brushing department as I should have been. So, the results were cavities. Several to be exact. I remember sitting in the waiting room listening to him drill and drill on some poor kid. To this day, I don't like going to the dentist. Odd to say, I would rather have my teeth pulled, than go to the dentist."

We both laughed, as I reached down to remove my wet socks. "Sorry, hope you don't mind."

"Certainly not," she said. "Go set them on the vent."

I strolled over to the vent, glancing at the new potted plants. "These are new?"

"Not really. They were there last time."

"Huh," I said, "could've sworn they were new." I sat back down on the couch, rubbing my toes to warm them up.

"Now, back to fears. You owe me one more," she said, clearing her throat.

"Are you grading me on these fears, like one to ten?"

"Not at all." She paused and smiled. "Maybe."

"Okay. My other fear is going in a strange bathroom that doesn't have a lock on the door. I fear I will be sitting on the toilet, and someone rushes in on me."

"Oh ... my ... God." She burst out laughing. "Jake, you are really screwed up."

We both laughed 'til tears came down our faces. She handed me a tissue, and we blew in unison.

"Okay. That was fun," she said. "Thanks, I needed that."

"Needed what—to know my fears or to laugh?"

"Both. I needed them both," she paused to blow her nose. "All right, let's get back on track. How are the dreams?"

"Good. I haven't had that dream in a month or so. I am beginning to have lots of sex dreams, though." I smiled. "Maybe you cured me?"

She smiled. "I don't cure people, Jake. They cure themselves." She ignored the sex comment.

"Does that mean I get a break on the bill?" I asked.

"Not a chance."

"Worth a try."

An uncomfortable silence crept into the room and sat between us. She tapped her pen on her spiral notebook without looking at me, as I played with a loose thread from my pants. After a few silent seconds, she lifted her head.

"Let's start today with life at home. Sometime ago, in our early sessions, you said you felt detached from Joan. What did you mean by that?"

"Well, I am not certain I know how to answer that."

"Are you happy, Jake?" she asked, tucking her feet beneath her. "Really, happy?"

"No, I'm not. It's not that she doesn't try, but I know I need to get better before our marriage will get better."

"Do you have an active sex life?" she asked.

"Not really," I said. "That life moved to holidays and birthdays. Part of it is me, I know. I'm simply not interested, for whatever reason. Sometimes we argue about sex, and that argument will lead to others."

"Give me an example of your last argument about sex."

This might be awkward.

"Mel, I am not sure how to . . . well, look, our last argument was about my not wanting to have sex."

"Why didn't you?" she asked. "Were you tired? Sometimes, we fall into a ditch in our sex lives. Many times it is hard to climb out."

"No, that's not it." I reached down for my cup of tea and sipped—buying time.

"Then . . . what?"

"She was having her monthly time."

"She was menstruating," she said.

"Yes. She said that if I loved her, it wouldn't make a difference to me. It was simple as that."

"From there an argument?"

"Something like that," I said.

"Why does she think it's simple?"

"I don't know. Maybe she has talked with her friends. Got a read on how their husbands react."

"Have you always had this issue?"

"Yes. I don't understand why, but I have," I said.

"We have talked about your dream and your recollection of what happened to you a long time ago. But, you have never spoken of what happened at the end. What did you do after she was done with you?"

"Nothing. I was afraid to do anything. But I remember feeling sick to my stomach."

"Did you lie there all night? Did you get up?"

"No. I got up a few hours later. I couldn't stand…well…the smell. I felt dirty."

Mel looked me in the eyes. She knew why, but she would hang back until I grew the spine to say it.

"Smell?" she asked, her legs coming out from under her. She sat on the edge of her chair. "What smell?"

"When I snuck out of the room, all I wanted to do was wash my hands. My hands had this bad smell. Like death, you know. I went to the bathroom and quietly shut the door not wanting to wake anyone."

"Go on. What did you do then?"

"There was a light beside the sink. I switched it on."

"What happened when you switched the light on?" she asked, eyes not blinking.

"Blood," I felt sick at my stomach.

She didn't move. Her eyes waited.

"Blood," she said. Not a question.

"My hands were covered in dried blood."

CHAPTER FOURTEEN

The Talk

(1974)

IN THE SUMMER BEFORE MY SENIOR YEAR, I worked two jobs—a bagger over at Mixon's Grocery and a welder at Dad's plant. I was saving for a car and college and needed the dough. Dad and I had our eyes on a two-door Buick Skylark. Green with nice wheels. It ran sweet and didn't need a lot of work, maybe a little paint here or there. The old Chevy had seen her last mile of asphalt. A few months ago, we had her towed off for the parts. I loved that car. Kinda like your first girlfriend. No matter who you end up with, the first girl always has a special place in your heart.

"Jake, get up. We have a lot to do today, young man," Dad yelled. I could hear him tapping the pot with the wooden spoon. Bing, bing, bing. "Daylight's a burning."

Dad was born with calluses on both hands and energy for hard work. He was short, thin with a deep tanned face that spoke of a life outdoors. His hair was gray, nose long and straight, and when he smiled, you knew it.

"Oh, okay. I'm getting up," I yelled back. How does he wake up in such a good mood EVERY day?

"Jake! You awake?" That was so old, and he was so deaf. One more year, and I am outta here, I thought.

"Dad, lose the spoon and pot, okay. I'm on my way," I yelled, crawling to the edge of my bed. I stood and walked to the bathroom and froze in front of the mirror. My blond hair was shaggy long and looked as if two squirrels had wrestled in it during the night. I grabbed my feed store cap and pulled it down low. The locks will be gone next week. Football. Coach didn't like long hair. Actually, Coach didn't like hair at all.

I knew Dad had been up since before the chickens. He'd make coffee and pace the house waiting for the right time to wake us. If it were up to him, he would have rolled me out of bed an hour ago. Mom often helped out in that department.

"Let him sleep a bit longer," she'd say. "This is his last year at home, and he'll be off to college. I want it to be a good year for Jake."

It wasn't that Dad wanted to work me like the Amish. He liked to talk early in the morning. During hunting season, we would wake at the butt crack of dawn. Dressed in our long johns and coveralls, we'd sit under a tree waiting for a big buck to step out into the open. But, before we would leave for the woods, we would just talk around the kitchen table. He would tell us about when he was a young boy growing up on this farm.

We hunted a lot growing up, but we rarely killed anything. We shot at cans, trees, fence posts, and whiskey bottles. You name it. Dad was serious about his hunting, though. My brother and I just liked being with him.

"Jake, are you coming or not?" he yelled. "I'm gonna put your keys in my pocket for the week if you don't get rolling."

"Coming." Geez, I'm dying here. "I'm washing up."

I pulled on my gym shorts and a Steppenwolf T-shirt and jogged outside. It was barely 7 a.m., and the heat sat on us like a thick blanket. I grabbed one of the large buckets and set off for the garden. The rows seem to get longer every year. There were rows and rows of butter beans, peas, corn, okra, and squash. He even planted a row of yams. I love yams. Not sure why, but I love 'em.

Our routine was the same. He would take one row. I would take the one next to him. We would pick and talk. Pick and talk. Our best days were spent in those dusty rows, talking mostly about nothing.

"You got big plans tonight, son?" he asked, tossing a handful of butter beans into the plastic pail.

"I'm taking Joan to a movie over at the Triangle."

"Yeah?"

"Yeah," I said. "We might drive over to the Dinner Bell and grab a burger or something before."

"Ole Marge really knows how to make a burger, don't she? I think her secret's in the bun," he said.

"I don't know, Dad. It must be somethin'. The service stinks."

I asked, "What about you guys? Doing anything special? It's Saturday night, you know."

"Gonna drive over to Bert's and pick up a brisket to cook out on the grill. I think Granny is coming over to eat with us. For a skinny old lady, she can eat like a linebacker."

"You better tune up your loud voice, if Granny's coming over," I said. "Sounds like a swinging night at the Travis grill."

He grunted a laugh, stood and peeped over into my row. "Jake, make sure you don't forget to turn those butter bean plants over. The beans hide underneath, you know. Half the time, I gotta go behind you and pick what you missed."

"Yep, got it," I shrugged and rolled my eyes.

"Don't roll your eyes, Jake." He looked over into my row.

I stood, kicked my pail a few feet, and faced him. "How in the world did you see my eyes roll?" I asked.

"I wiped your butt when you were a baby. I know all things."

"How in the world does wiping my butt have anything to do with rolling my eyes?"

"You ever wipe someone's butt, Jake?"

"God, no."

"Well, when you do, you'll know what I'm talking about. Until then, pull the beans from underneath the plant," he said.

"Okay, okay. Still not sure what butt wiping has to do with anything."

"Do you need any money? I might have a few dollars if you need it." He reached into his jean's pocket and retrieved his wallet. He opened it and snapped it shut without saying a word. Mom may have picked his pocket when he wasn't looking.

"No, Dad. I got paid last Friday, so, I'm flush with cash at the moment. Thank you, though."

"You and Joan have been going out a lot lately. You guys like each other, huh?"

That was about as forward as Dad got. He was not an outwardly emotional guy. His entire generation seemed to be that way. We rarely talked about girls or love, or anything remotely connected. Butt wiping was a new one for us.

"She and I like each other okay. Maybe…a little more than okay," I said, reaching down and turning the plant on its side, wondering if a big water moccasin was underneath waiting to take a bite out of me.

"Really?" He stood and looked at me, arching his back, working out the morning kinks. "A little more than okay?" He returned to his plant, reached down, and pulled a large weed from beneath the bean plant, shaking the dirt off before tossing it to the side.

"This year will be a big year for you, Jake. Thinking about playing college ball?"

"Like to, but not sure if I'm good enough."

"Oh, you're good enough, Jake. Not sure you're big enough. The game at the college level is faster and bigger."

"I might try to walk on. I don't think I'll get a scholarship offer though, not from Texas, I won't."

"You're probably right 'bout that," he said. "They got their pick of the big city blue-chippers."

We picked in silence for a while, kicking our buckets down the row. Something was eating at him; I could tell.

"Old man Shaw's gonna dig himself a big lake in the back pasture."

"Yeah?" I said. "Maybe he will stock it with some largemouth bass."

He didn't say anything.

"Going to Texas is going to be expensive, Dad. The tuition is double most other schools around here. Austin is more expensive to live in as well."

"You know, I was wondering about that. Money is tight, son, especially with your little brother and sister still at home," he said. "How are we gonna manage all of this?"

"I'll work all summer and save. If I can get on at the plant, I'll have my tuition for the first semester. I'm planning on getting a job once I get to Austin. I can work and take a full load. I know I can."

"I'll help where I can. You know, books and stuff. Okay?" He handed me a fresh bucket and turned back to his row.

I watched him tearing at the plant for every last bean. "Dad, things will be fine. I'm not worried."

We both knew I was worried. Moving from a small town to a large city is scary. Enrolling in a university that has forty thousand kids is damn frightening. I was worried enough for both of us.

"What kind of team we gonna have this year? ZeDonks going all the way?" he asked.

"Well, we lost a lot of players last year. Depends who shows up this year."

"Jake, you know, you're the first Travis to go to college. We're mighty proud of you, son. I hope that you know that."

I stopped and looked at his back as he walked toward the barn. He worked hard his entire life. His family never gave him anything but a hard time. Dad had big shoulders, and he's always needed them.

I turned my plant over and dug deep into the base, determined to find every last bean.

I thought for a minute.

I whispered, "I know, Dad...I know." I could feel the stress piling on.

I glanced at my watch. Getting late. I needed to pick up the pace, or I would be picking beans well into my date tonight. I pulled my bucket alongside and began to shake the bushes for beans and dig deep for the ones hiding from me. I finished my row and had started the last one.

"Son, could I speak with you?" Dad yelled from inside the barn.

"I'm on my last row. Can it wait until I get through?"

"Why don't you stop now? That row and the other two between you and the fence were planted late, so those can wait. Likely 'til next weekend."

"Why didn't you tell me that when we started?" I yelled back, standing to stretch.

I gathered my buckets and walked to the barn. I could see Dad at the other end of the barn, near the stalls, sharpening a new blade for his tiller. On my way over to him, pail in hand, I stopped and poured the contents into a large container, certain that Mom and Dad will likely end up spending their evening watching All in the Family and shelling beans. Life on a farm.

"Why didn't you tell me about that row of beans when we start-ed?" I asked again.

"I find it interesting to watch you work when there is a girl waiting for you at the end of the day." He smiled.

I smiled back. "What's up in here?"

Dad pressed his forefinger to his mouth. "Shush." He reached into a wooden toolbox that held his larger blades and wrenches. He turned and showed me a magazine.

A Playboy magazine.

"Your mom found this in your room," he said, handing it to me, with the monthly Playgirl foldout dangling. "Along with this can of Skoal."

My speech was slow to develop.

"Well?" he insisted. "Is this the kind of trash I've taught you to read?"

"No, Dad it's not." I handed the magazine back to him, with a sheepish grin growing on my face. "I don't read it."

He seized the magazine from me, opened it, and scanned a few of the photo layouts. I followed his eyes from one to another. He even turned the magazine up to see the fold-out of the month. He pushed it back at me.

"Well, okay. Good talk, Jake."

He smiled, turned, and went back to his work, leaving me standing there. "Have a nice time, tonight. Don't be late. And in the future, store your girlie stuff out here. Here's a lock." He tossed me a large Binfield lock with a key in it. "I emptied an old toolbox for you. Your things will be safe here."

I nodded thanks and bolted out.

As I hiked the trail leading to the house, it occurred to me that this was only the second time in my life Dad had spoken to me about sex. I mean, I wasn't asking for a lecture on the methods of procreation, but maybe some advice might be in order. Tossing me a lock and telling me to store my magazines in his toolbox did not qualify as an educational forum, but it was as close as I might get.

The first time Dad had any words remotely connected to sex was before my first date, two years ago. And I had to dig hard to find it in that conversation. He just didn't feel comfortable talking about it.

Of course, I learned all of the basics from Smitty and the gang. And I could also always count on the boys' restroom doors to contain ample suggestions, some with phone numbers.

I smiled to myself remembering that conversation with Dad, as I stopped by the well house and poured a cold glass of water. Sitting down on a deer hide stool, I giggled when I thought about his feeble attempt at sex education. It happened a couple of years ago.

I had spent all day long cleaning the Chevy to a sparkle. The tires and rims had been freshly scrubbed, seats vacuumed, and springs adequately moved. I had a date with Sara and hoped she preferred me over bad seats.

I was about to leave. "Who's got the keys? They're not on the board." I yelled to no one in particular. "I need to stop and gas up. Need to leave…like, now."

I walked through the house. My little brother and sister were over at their friends. Mom and Dad were no were to be found.

"In here, Jake," Dad said. "We're in the living room."

"Oh, there you are." I stood in the hallway, peering into the room.

There sat Mom and Dad positioned in the middle of the living room couch. This room was built with the original house but seldom used. The furniture was formal and uncomfortable, with two straight back chairs and a pullout sofa that no one was allowed to drink or eat on. Actually, food was not allowed past the door frame. There was no television, which was a big negative. The room was conveniently turned into a place where we had family meetings. Our grades were reviewed in this room. Punishment for offenses was delivered from this room. Mom and Dad often fought in this room.

So, I was a bit nervous when I stepped into the room and saw them sitting there, holding hands like they were about to hear bad news like a "C" in algebra.

"What's up? Do you have the keys to the car?" I asked, checking my pockets for my wallet.

"Mom and I would like to visit with you before you leave," Dad said, his toe tapping the cheap carpet.

As if it were her cue, Mom stood, gave Dad the eye, and casually walked out of the room, shutting the sliding doors behind her. I noticed she held the keys to the car in her left hand, dangling them as she exited.

"What's up?" I asked. "What's Mom doing with the keys?"

"Mom and I thought I should talk with you before you leave." His leg jumped in rhythm with his toes.

"Sure. What does Mom want you to talk to me about?"

"Why don't you sit for a minute?" he asked. "This won't take long," he crossed his legs and tapped the arm of the couch.

I complied and sat in the stiff straight back chair across from him.

His eyes fixed on the drapery material behind me and gradually moved to the plastic tree next to me. Finally, they rested on his worn work boots. He bent forward, his elbows resting on his knees, his hands clasped in a death grip. His eyes remained on his boots.

"Well, Jake. This is your first time out on a real date. There are a lot of responsibilities that go along with that."

"You need to watch your speed. We don't need any tickets," he said. "Make sure you open the door for the young lady."

I sat there looking at him studying a stain on his boots.

"Well, Mom and I wanted to make sure you knew how to be a gentleman. You should take that responsibility seriously. We do." He cleared his throat.

"Okay." Silence swarmed the room. I waited for him to take the next move, but it was painful to see him struggle. I glanced at my watch. "Dad, can we get on with it? I'm gonna be late."

"Yes, of course." He stood and walked to the end of the room, seemingly talking to himself, and turned to face me. "Keep the thing in its house." He exhaled, sat down on the couch, and looked me in the eyes. "Keep the thing in its house, Jake. A lot of bad things can happen if you don't do that."

"Dad, what on earth are you talking about? What is this thing you keep referring to?" I asked. "What house?"

His eyes sought the refuge of the draperies again, then the plant and finally back to his boots.

"Dad, are you talking about sex?" I asked, grinning.

"Shush, Jake, not so loud. Mom's gonna hear you. She wanted me to explain the birds and the bees. She would split a gut if she thought we were in here talking about sex."

I looked at him. "Dad, at school we had classes on this whole topic." I reached over and patted his knee. "I think I understand the symbolism here, so let's leave it at that. Plus, most of my sex education came from Smitty anyway."

"That's what your mom's afraid of."

I sat there, waiting.

"Great. Good talk." He stood and gave me a hug. "Now, have a nice time with Sara."

As I opened the door and walked out of the room, Dad stayed behind to wipe the perspiration off his forehead. Mom held the keys out for me as I turned to leave. "Have a nice time, Jake. I know you will. I saw Sara's mom at the beauty parlor last weekend. Oh, I don't know if we told you, but Dad and I saw Sara's parents at the Travis cemetery cleaning last month."

I was grabbing my jacket. "What were her parents doing at a Travis family cemetery work day?" I slipped into my jacket and started out the door. "Must have been a volunteer group from one of the other churches, huh?"

Mom walked to the door as I was inspecting the shine on the chrome windows. "No, Jake. She is your cousin. On her mom's side."

She started her genealogy recital and placed a finger near her forehead to think.

I held the door open to the Chevy. One hand on my hip said it all.

"What? My…cousin?" I asked. "That's a bit disturbing."

"Yes, darling. She's your second cousin, twice removed, I think…or …oh I don't know. I get so confused with the first removed or second removed. Do you remember how that works?"

"Mom, you're telling me Sara's my cousin?"

"She's a lovely girl, isn't she?" She waved to me as I slammed the door shut. "…Oh and don't be late taking her home. Her daddy collects guns and likes to use them. Have fun, Jake."

CHAPTER FIFTEEN

Session Nineteen

(December 2004)

I RUSHED FROM NORDSTROM with my newly wrapped package, dodging a Santa bell ringer who smelled of hard liquor and long hours. Needed to hurry, or I would be late for my session with Mel. So far, I had a perfect record to date and didn't want to ruin it. White lights draped the trees lining the road, giving it a holiday luster. Houses were decorated with Christmas fare. Earlier in the day, there was a dusting of snow. What would the season be without snow.

Guiding my car into the tight parking space reserved for patients, I popped the trunk and retrieved the package. I noticed her parking place was empty, which was not completely unusual. Sometimes Mel rode with her husband, who was an internist practicing in the adjacent building. I climbed the outer stairs two at a time, pulled open the glass doors, and hiked down the long hallway. Standing at the exterior door, I rang the patient's bell—twice.

Nothing.

Maybe she went to the ladies' room. I waited a few more minutes and rang again.

Nothing.

After twenty minutes, I stopped ringing the bell and worry took hold of me. Mel had never missed a session. If a conflict arose, she would always call to change the day or time. Could she have been in an accident? I looked around. It was almost 4:30. I marched down the hall, grabbed a pay phone, and called my office.

No messages from Mel.

I wandered back outside and looked around. Finally, I pulled my coat around my ears and sat on the concrete steps.

"Jake," a voice behind me said.

I turned and jumped up. "Jake, I am so sorry. Please come in." She held the door for me, and we trekked down to her office. She unlocked the door and switched on the light. That was when I noticed it. She looked bad. Her cheeks were gray and her eyes sunken. All of a sudden, she was fragile.

"Are you okay?" I asked. "I was worried about you."

"Of course you were. I'm fine. I got stuck in a meeting at the hospital regarding a patient. I'm very sorry to keep you waiting like this. It's not like me to be so frazzled."

"Everything all right?" I moved a stack of books from the couch.

She stared at me, then to the rug. She was searching for inspiration in the same spot I had been for months.

"No, Jake. Everything's not okay."

"Well, do you want to talk about it? We don't have to do my thing today. I'm much better. No bad dreams or anything. Let me be your therapist today."

She smiled. "Jake, that's not a good idea, at all. Maybe we should just reschedule for another day."

"Wait...then...let me be your friend."

She sat completely still. "All right, be my friend."

"I'll make you tea. After months of watching you make tea, I think I got it down," I said. "Here, sit tight."

"Thank you." Mel reached over and pulled a thick blanket around her shoulders and tucked her legs underneath. I could feel her eyes on me as I moved about.

I hustled up the tea bags and started the pot of water. I grabbed her sugar and the milk. Found her serving set and placed it all neatly in the center. I poured the water into the cups and carried the server to the coffee table.

We both sipped in silence.

"Oh, I almost forgot—bought you a Christmas present." I picked up the wrapped package and placed it in her lap. "Open it."

"That was not necessary, and if I recall, is definitely against all protocols for therapy."

"Come on. It's not a big deal. I wanted to get you something. Really more as a thank you than a Christmas present."

"You know I'm Jewish, right?"

"So was Jesus." I smiled. "Open it."

She lifted the package and shook it.

"Well, it's not breakable." I sat my cup and saucer on the table.

As she ripped the paper from the small box, I felt a sense of deep gratitude. Mel Allen was my therapist and my best friend. I'm not sure how those reconciled in the annals of psychotherapy, but I didn't care.

She smiled as she lifted the top and peered inside. "Socks!"

"They're almost as wild and crazy as the others you wear, but I can assure you, Janis Joplin would be proud to wear them on her feet."

"Thank you, Jake. That's very kind and thoughtful."

I sat there finishing my tea as she returned the multicolored socks to their box, slowly replacing the top on the box. After a second, she set it aside and looked over at me.

"Do you remember your graduation from high school?" she asked.

"Like it was yesterday," I smiled. "Smitty Grinds went commando and mooned the crowd when he got his diploma. We had a bet."

"Well, do you remember the feeling you had when you walked across the podium and received your diploma?"

"You mean the shock and amazed feeling or the one of being … free?" I smiled and reached for my cup, careful to not spill my tea.

"I think I mean the one where you felt free."

"Yes, I remember that feeling, but I repressed it because I was scared shitless."

She set her cup down on the end table and gazed at me.

"Jake. You need to think about graduation, and soon."

"Mel, I'm not sure I follow you." I noticed she didn't have her notebook. No pen in hand.

"At some point, you will need to graduate from my class," she said. "You can't just do this for the rest of your life."

"Okay. Tell me what that means."

"Graduation from my class implies you will need to sit down with your mom and dad and tell them what happened to you. All of it."

"What if I'm not ready? I don't think I'm ready for that, yet. I mean, I haven't even told Joan about this."

"You will need to tell them all in order to be free, especially Joan."

"Mel, I need more time to work through this. I need you to listen to …" I stopped and stared at her. "Why do you think I need to do this now?"

"Jake, I intend to close my practice." She wrapped her arms around her chest, pulling the blanket tighter against her body.

"What? Why?" I asked. "You have a full load of patients. What's happened?"

"We need to work on getting you to graduate. I'll arrange another therapist who will pick up my load afterward."

"What? I don't want another therapist. You're my gal." I stood and walked over to the window. The freeway was locked in holiday traffic, and I felt like I was losing control.

"You should not talk to your therapist like that. I'm..." She fought the tears.

We sat in silence for a long while, searching for answers in that cheap rug.

"Mel, I don't know what's wrong, but I've cried on this couch and spilled my life to you in this room. You know more about me than anyone. Please don't let me walk out of here like that. Please. Let me help."

She stared over at the window, pulled the blanket from around her shoulders, and began to fold it neatly. "Merry Christmas, Jake."

I stood, grabbed my coat, and stopped as I reached the door.

"I'll call your service after the holidays and schedule, okay?" I paused to see if she was listening.

She simply nodded.

I walked outside and sank down on the steps. It was dark, and there were a few flakes of snow falling around.

Maybe all of this was my fault.

I heard a noise behind me. A door opening. It was Mel. Wrapped in her blanket, she sat down beside me. She looked to the sky and then over to me.

"It's not your fault." She reached for my hand and squeezed it tight. "I have Stage 4 breast cancer. They have told me at best, I have six months, maybe longer. It's going to be a hard road for me."

We sat there in the snow and chill and held hands.

And cried.

CHAPTER SIXTEEN

G.I. JOE

(1974)

I PULLED MY CHEVY INTO THE GRAVEL PARKING LOT, shut off the engine, and watched as the kids filed one by one through the main door. Our new principal, Joe Folk, stood outside and welcomed the newcomers. He was tall, lanky, and sported a toothy grin beneath closely cropped hair—hence, the nickname, "G.I. Joe." His head sat on a swivel and moved at a constant rate from kid to kid, as he greeted each one. I smiled to myself. I gave him a full month before he was overcome with the urge to commit murder.

The incoming freshmen looked like abandoned fawns in the woods. Definitely too young to be in high school.

Seniors were given priority over all class schedules, but seniors who happened to play football were considered special. My first class of the morning was study hall, which just so happened to be my favorite class. Only on rare occasions did we actually study in study hall. The teacher in charge knew the game and pretty much left us to our own devices.

I marched into the large open room, making a beeline for the lockers. There was a flurry of hall activity around me. Backpacks getting stowed. Books hitting the tables. The sound of chairs being moved closer to someone of the opposite sex.

"Good morning, Jake," the loud voice echoed. "You need to pick up your class schedule at the principal's office. Pronto." Betty Posten was a heavy-set lady with thin hair and the face of an English bulldog, but we loved her like our own mothers. She was, let's say, extremely toler-ant with our extracurricular activities. She covered for us when the office Nazis would circulate the halls looking for detention candidates.

"Thanks, Mrs. Posten. You're the best…still." I waved to her desk as I scurried to my table.

"Keep 'em coming pretty boy and you just might graduate from this prison camp," she said.

"Yes ma'am. I expanded my repertoire of Mrs. Posten compli-ments over the summer. Even took a night class. My aim is to turn your face red," I said.

"Well, for God's sake, don't wait until end of the year to dish 'em out. Could be too late."

"Okay." I skidded to a stop to say hello to one of the lovelies up front.

"By the way, the bell rang three minutes ago, lover boy. If you don't want to spend your first day in detention hall, I suggest you kick it in high gear," Mrs. Posten said.

"Yes, ma'am. On my way." I gave her a solid salute.

I hustled to my locker and threw my books and binders in the clut-tered bin. Then, I pulled out my ZeDonk play book and made it to my study table before the tardy bell announced trouble.

There they sat at the same table. The two of them, like they never left last May.

"Don't you guys want to maybe change things up just a bit this year?" I said. "It's our senior year, you know. Let's live dangerously."

"Why should we change up anything?" Hicker Nutt asked. "We've sat at this table for three whole years."

"My point exactly." I glanced down at the chair backs. "Not only have we occupied this very table, we have sat in these exact chairs," I said, pointing at the date carvings left over the years by each of us. "Why don't we move up, or over, or back or something?"

Smitty Grinds looked at me with furrowed brow. "I like where I sit. Happy as a puppy with two peckers." He gestured across the hallway. "Got a good chance of shooting my panty limit from this angle. I can see right up Cheryl's dress from right here. Lookie there. No siree. I ain't moving nowhere. That's one short dress, huh? More like a short T-shirt."

Hicker and I glanced across the hall into Mrs. Krouse's Chemistry class. There sat Cheryl Black pretending to be oblivious to the three of us gawking at her white panties. It sure was a short dress.

He had my attention. "More like a handkerchief, Smitty. A pocket square at most," I said.

Cheryl was a great looking girl. Blonde, big, round blue eyes, shapely legs, and a round ass. I could picture her seeking advanced degrees in The Art of Male Teasing. She glanced over our way, gave us a big smile, and crossed her tanned legs in slow motion. We all scooted our chairs to the edge of the table and stared into the Chemistry 101 class. Sitting shoulder to shoulder and cheek to cheek, we patiently waited for her next move. It took about a minute. She glanced over and delighted us once again with a reverse cross-over. There they were. Panties. White. Praise the Lord.

"Did you see that?" Smitty laughed and pointed.

"Did I see what?" A voice, deep and irritated caught us off guard.

Our heads shot upward. There he was G.I. Joe. The principal freak of nature. He was 6 feet, 8 if he was an inch, and from where we sat, he looked much taller. "You boys interested in Chemistry, huh?" The three of us looked at each other. Busted.

"Or is it anatomy that you prefer?" he said, placing his massive hands on his hips. "Or perhaps you three stooges want hunting season to start early. I heard something about shooting your limit."

I opened my mouth to apologize, but before I could breathe a word, Smitty was off and running.

"Yessir, Mr. Folk. Loved chemistry. Took it last year," he said. "Actually, you may not know this about me, but I'm a student of the sciences." We all turned in our chairs to face the giant. Smitty, however, was on a roll and needed to stop. I searched for a leg to kick.

"Why is it we can only take Chemistry 101 only once?" Smitty asked. "There ought to be some rule where if'n you really like a class, and you excelled in it, you could take it again. I mean, what if I decide I want to be a doctor? Science class just might be something I could use, you know."

Mr. Folk eyed all of us like he was looking down a gun barrel, but finally rested his disdain on Smitty, who had cleanly broken a Guinness record of shoveling shit. The old Marine was capable of snapping each of our heads from our shoulders with one hand. I suspected he memorized each of our files. He knew that the closest place Smitty would be to a college would be working the lawns or mopping the hallways. "Well, Smitty, if my memory serves me, you squeaked by Chemistry 101. I think you made a D, didn't you? Also, that F in Biology could place a hamper on that medical career you seek," he said.

Hicker giggled and punched me in the shoulder.

"Yessir, that Mrs. Krouse didn't like me much in Chemistry," Smitty said, giving Hicker the evil eye, "and that Biology class was a complete waste of time. What's an amoeba got to do with curing stuff like cancer or the clap?"

"Tell you what. You boys turn your chairs around and face the front of Mrs. Posten's class." As the giant moved to leave, he paused, "Smitty, why don't you stop by my office later? Maybe I can find a way that you can take Chemistry 101 all over again. What'dya say?"

"Well, huh. Um, yessir," Smitty said.

I wanted to tell Smitty that just because Mr. Folk is new doesn't mean he's stupid. Smitty's school rap sheet was longer than his junior class paper. He was on every teacher's watch list for dishing out loads of bullshit.

Mr. Folk bent down into our space and whispered through clenched teeth, "You boys have a nice day and a great senior year, but let me be perfectly clear. My office sits about fifteen feet on the other side of that wall. Because of my height, I can hear a frog fart in the next county. Be careful."

He smiled at us and walked off, giving a wave to Mrs. Posten, who looked embarrassed and pissed that we got busted on her watch.

"Holy fuck. We're in trouble. Deep trouble," Hicker whispered. "Where on earth did they find this guy?"

I watched Mr. Folk as he marched back to his office. "The Marine Corps, boys. The U. S. Marine Corps."

Smitty looked at us both, oblivious to reality. "I don't know about you two, but I think he likes me."

I glanced at Smitty and shook my head.

CHAPTER SEVENTEEN

The Heartbeat of a Team

(1974)

"YOU GIRLS don't deserve to wear the ZeDonk jersey. I'm surprised you have the balls to wear it on Friday nights," Coach Jenkins yelled, as tobacco spit hammered the boys in the huddle. "Get your head out of your ass; pull those skirts up high and tight, 'cause you're running 'til they turn the lights on!"

The first two months of fall passed at the speed of paint drying on a fence post. The ZeDonk's football season was turning out to be a nightmare, and the teachers, now a branch of the United States Marine Corps, were relentless in their assignments and grading. It wasn't going to be as easy as we hoped. Between football practice and class assignments, most of us normal students had little time left over for real educational activities, like climbing the forestry tower or scribbling notes to our latest love.

The ZeDonk's record for the previous three years stood at twenty-eight wins and two losses. Both losses were close games, but fierce battles in the state championship. This year, we were winless—beaten up and trounced every Friday night. Even our homecoming game was an embarrassment. We couldn't beat a girl's volleyball team if they suited up across from us.

And the more we lost, the harder our coaches pushed us during practice.

Coach Jenkins wanted to prove a point about our game, or lack thereof, so he instructed one of the assistant coaches to purchase twenty-five large dresses from the local charity. In the locker room, he passed them out to each of us. We stood there in shock and shame.

"Yo, Coach, you expect me to wear this dress outside?" someone yelled. "That's kinda sicko, don't you think?"

"No, Reggie. Why don't you simply turn your equipment in now and save us all the time," he replied. Reggie hid behind his locker and seemed unsure of his next step. Ten minutes later, he tossed his equipment into the cage and bolted like he was late for a date.

As for the rest of us, we took the field and ran offensive and defensive plays wearing skirts and dresses. Mine was a cute blue dress with lace around the collar. It was difficult for us seniors to hold our head up, but the freshmen seemed to enjoy it.

Coach was true to his word. We ran laps 'til dark dressed like we were going to the prom. I hoped the coaching staff would grow tired of the degradation and let us go home, but my hopes vanished when the stadium lights were turned on.

Coach blew his whistle and motioned for us to gather in the center of the field. "Take a knee," he said. "It's been a tough year for all of us. We are 0 and 5. Your season is half over, and the toughest conference games lie ahead. The seniors on this team have lost two games in their career. And it is because of the blood they spilled on this field that we need to make some changes. The time is now to find out who is committed to playing the rest of the year. Win or lose. I don't care. What I do care about is giving each practice and each game all you got. If you'll do that, each and every one of you will be winners in my book. Talent is not your problem, men. It's the attitude of some that has poisoned the hearts of this team." He paused and looked around. Not a player moved.

He spit to the turf. He peered at each face. Coach was drawing a line in the sand.

We were exhausted, sweated down, and bloodied. "If you want to play on this team, you'll get up and run until I turn these lights off. For those of you who are not committed, go inside and turn in your equipment to Coach LaGrone. There will be no questions asked."

All heads were bowed. Bodies rested on helmets. Sweat dripped from every player's hair. It didn't take me long. I knew what I needed to do. Without muttering a word, I stood up, pulled my head gear on, straightened my blue lace dress, and started jogging around the track. It was a lonely step. The sound of my cleats pushing through the dirt track echoed in the humid night. I was afraid to turn around. I kept my eyes focused on my next step, pushing my body to remain upright. I completed one lap, and I glanced to the center of the field. It was empty. No one was there.

I slowed my jog and stopped. There they were making the turn behind me, tugging at their dresses, and giving it all they had. I slapped them on the helmet as they ran past me, huffing, moaning and groaning. All twelve of them. This would be our team. That's all that mattered.

We lost half our team that night in the darkness of the ZeDonk stadium, but we recovered our honor. The team never looked back. What happened on the scoreboard would have little meaning in our life. What happened on the field that night would define us.

Before we made the second turn, the stadium went dark. We

slowed our jog to a stumble and started for the field house. Catching my breath, hands on my hips, I paused before I stepped into the field house. I searched for a sign of him. There he was, framed by the harvest moon, standing at the fifty. His arms were crossed, his head down.

Coach looked relieved.

With only thirteen players, most of them underclassmen, we had to be careful about injuries. All but two of us played offense and defense and never left the field once the game started. We had to learn new positions. Simplify the play book. We wore braces for leg injuries and taped hands for stitched cuts, but we never missed a game for the rest of the year.

Our last game was at home. It was against our arch rival Crosby Eagles. They were big, fast, and talented. The local newspaper predicted they would win the state championship. That night, the stands were packed. I remember looking at the faces from the end zone before we took the field. The crowd was behind us no matter the record. There was a charge in the air. I could feel it. We all felt it. If the Eagles wanted a perfect season, it would only come after blood was spilled on this field.

At half-time, we were tied 0 to 0. Our defense had come to play. Our offense lacked a running game, a passing attack, and we fumbled our opportunities away. So, unless we intercepted a pass and ran it back for a touchdown, we were likely going nowhere offensively. At half-time, we filed into the field house, hydrated, and sat down in a tight circle. Coach Jenkins stood in the middle.

"Men, I have never seen a better first half. We need to take care of the ball better and stop giving them opportunities. During the first half, we played a stacked blitz defense. The coaches and I have talked this over, and we are changing our defense for the second half. They will make changes to take advantage of the blitz, and we are going to surprise them with a new twist. Now, huddle up with your coach and get your new assignments." He paused and tossed some towels around. "Make sure you take your salt pills. We can't afford cramps."

We gathered our head gear and began to move to the position coaches. "Jake, come over here a minute."

"Yeah, Coach."

"I want you in the quarterback's pocket this second half. They know they can't run against our front four, but our secondary is young and inexperienced, and I think they are going to figure that out pretty soon."

"What do you want me to do?" I asked, wiping the sweat from my face with a towel.

"Get in his face, Jake. I mean every play. If he takes a shit, I want you standing there with the toilet paper. They can't catch a pass if he can't throw it. I want you to blitz every down. You got that? Every down."

"Got it." I stepped outside to cool off in the November breeze. A storm was on its way—I could smell the rain in the air. On the bench sat Smitty and Hicker. They looked exhausted. Black dirt stained their uniforms. Smitty had blood on his gloves. Both held their helmets between their legs.

I sat down beside them. "Hey guys."

"What did he want?" Hicker asked, pulling some tape off his hand.

"Suppose to wipe the quarterback's ass the second half. Blitz every down," I said, pulling some tape over my bloodied knuckle.

Smitty took a deep breath and let it out slowly. "Do you think we have a chance to beat these guys, Jake? I mean, I am getting my head handed to me up front. The fuckers are cheating, too. Guy grabs my jersey almost every play."

Hicker looked over. "Jake, my guy is fast. Real fast. I'm talking NFL fast. I couldn't cover him if I had a jet engine strapped to my ass."

"I know, Hicker. He signed with Texas last week. Their number one recruit. Do your best. All we can ask, right?" I said. "Smitty, knee that guard in the nuts the first play. You might get flagged, but I guarantee he won't hold you after that." I thought for a minute and turned to Hicker. "Don't let the wide receiver get off the line so quickly. Challenge him up front, at the line of scrimmage. Get aggressive. He's vain as hell. Doesn't like to wear a mouthpiece. On the first play, hit him square in the mouth. Searching the grass for his front teeth might slow him down a bit."

For the next few minutes, we sat in silence. In the distance, we could hear the ZeDonk fighting band playing a number. There was a pause and then the fight song. It sounded great, and I could feel the goose bumps on my arms. My last game on this field, and most likely, my last game forever.

If I don't remember anything else from this season, I will remember this moment, sitting with my best friends in the cool November night, bloodied but anxious to wage battle one last time. Seconds later, it began to rain and minutes later, the clouds opened.

You could hear some fans running for cover, while others came prepared. Within a minute, the entire stadium was covered with orange umbrellas. No one was leaving before this thing was over. I wanted to win this game for them. For me. But most of all, I wanted to win for Coach Jenkins.

The ZeDonks took the muddy field as the rain soaked our jerseys. We won the coin toss and chose to kickoff. My job on special teams was to break the wall of blockers in front of the runner. The object was to allow my teammates to have a shot once the wall was taken down. The role was not unlike a Kamikaze pilot. You aim your helmet at their chests and try to take as many down as you can.

Since it was our first kick-off opportunity of the night, I intended to make sure that those guys regretted coming onto this field. We might get our asses kicked, but the Eagles would know they traveled through ZeDonk stadium. They would not forget this night.

The kick was off, and it floated to the right side of the field to the ten-yard line. The ball was caught, and the back bolted to the center of the field searching for his blockers. I was flying low and could see the wall beginning to form. The anchorman was the middle blocker and was waiting for the running back to reach them before they pushed forward. He made a mistake and turned his head slightly searching for him, and that was when I made my move.

I felt my feet leave the ground as my facemask collided into the anchorman's chest, forcing him to fall backward into the runner. The half back was not expecting this, and he lost the handle, causing a fumble. There was a mass scramble for the football. Arms and legs searched beneath the mound. Screams and yells echoed. The whistle blew, and the refs began to pull us off the human heap, one by one.

There was a hush in the stands. All eyes watched the field, waiting for the referee to signal who had recovered the ball.

Three seconds later. Whistle. One player was found beneath the mess, Hicker Nutt, stood up with the ball, lifting it into the air. Ze-Donk ball. The home crowd burst into cheers, while the band played the fight song. The entire team rushed the field, and we huddled and pumped our fists high into the air.

I glanced up field. The Eagles' anchorman who took my hit kicked his helmet to the sideline, while his coach screamed into his face. The big guy turned to look at the celebration not ten yards from him. Blood trickled out of his nose. He pointed at me with his middle finger.

I smiled back. "You're not my type," I yelled.

For thirty minutes, we pounded each other relentlessly up and down the muddy field, but in the end, we succumbed to the talent and speed of the Eagles. The final score was 6 to 0.

When the final whistle blew, there was not an empty seat in the stands. No one left. They all stayed and cheered us on through the rain and the mud. Parents started to drift onto the field to hug and console their sons, while I walked to the Eagles sideline in search of the anchorman. Our eyes finally met. He walked to meet me. I stopped and held my right hand out.

"Good luck next week. You guys played a hell of a game," I said.

"Thanks." He glanced over to the bench. "I'm sorry about my reaction earlier. It was a clean hit. My ears are still ringing." He smiled, slapped my helmet, and began to walk to their field house. I started the trip over to our bench.

I remember feeling more proud of wearing my ZeDonk jersey that night than at any time before. Sometimes, we learn more about ourselves in defeat than we ever do during victory. The Coach had been trying so hard to teach us that one lesson all season. I smiled to myself as it, like the rain, soaked in.

The drizzle slowed as the temperature dipped. I could see Mom and Dad huddled in a blanket underneath their orange umbrella waving at me. Dad gave me the fist pump sign. Mom was shivering. I waved and searched the sideline for my helmet and gear. Finding what I needed, I started for the dressing room.

I didn't jog off the field this night, but took my time. I wanted to absorb it all just one last time.

"Jake," he called from behind me. Coach Jenkins caught up beside me and placed his arm around my shoulder pads, giving me a hug. "Jake, I have coached a lot of great players over the years. Many of them you played with. But, I want you to know I've never coached anyone with a bigger heart."

I stopped to look at him. He seemed to have aged ten years during this season. He reached up and rubbed my wet hair. "I could always count on you to give it your all," he said. "Thanks, Jake. It was an honor."

He turned, speaking to other players. I stood there watching him give something of meaning to each one—words of encouragement, a hug, a pat on the butt for others. But no one left that field not knowing how he felt about us, not as a team, but as individuals.

The words he spoke lived inside of me. They grew roots, and during the long years of doubt and fear ahead of me, it was this moment and these words that sustained me.

CHAPTER EIGHTEEN

The Last Session

IT WAS 3:50 IN THE AFTERNOON. I parked the car in my usual spot and walked up the stairs to Mel's building. I held the door for a couple of movers who were carting out boxes labeled with green and white tags. They appeared to have been at it a while, as several taped boxes sat near the entrance to be loaded into the moving van. The overweight guy seemed to be struggling with the day's work. His shirt showed perspiration, and his breathing was labored. It was February, and the weather was unseasonably warm. People walked about enjoying the last of the day's sunshine. I knew this day would come, but I dreaded it and silently hoped she would ring me telling me it was all a big mistake, and she would be all right.

I overheard the fat man say, "Joe, Tom, let's take a break. The doctor lady said that she'd be busy with appointments until 5:30. Let's go grab some coffee over at Luke's Diner."

The other two looked at him with relief and tossed the boxes on the cart and started for the diner that was located nearby. "Thank God. These books are freaking heavy," one said. "No kidding," the skinny guy agreed.

I let the front entrance door slide to a close and watched them drift over to Luke's. I could smell the coffee from where I stood. Nobody makes it better or stronger than Luke.

The door to Mel's outer office was held open by a screwdriver tucked beneath. I yanked it out and looked for a place to put it down. There was none. The room was empty. No waiting chairs. No cheap paintings on the wall. Even the plastic plants had been boxed and carted out. So, I stood there with the tool in hand and waited for Mel to arrive.

After a few minutes the door to her personal office opened.

"Jake, come in. Oh my God, you're early!"

"Very...funny. Well, I figured since I was your last patient, I wanted to get my money's worth." I smiled.

"Really?" Mel said, laughing. She let the door swing shut and shuffled to her chair in her house shoes, grabbing the screwdriver and dropping it on top of a labeled box.

Mel's clothes made her seem small now, and she looked like she was about to go for a long stroll in a frozen tundra. Her long skirt was replaced with heavy cords and a thick, plaid, wool shirt. The chemotherapy had taken its toll on her body. Her ashen face told the story. Mel had undergone a double mastectomy two months ago, and she looked it.

The room was barren save for two chairs, a small coffee table, and the tea service. I walked over to the teapot and started our ritual. She sat down in her chair and curled her legs beneath her body, crossing her arms over her chest. She was either chilled or self-conscious of the damage.

The rugs were rolled, taped, and stood against the wall. Boxes were neatly labeled and stacked in the corner of the room. Even in this condition, Mel was particular with how her things would be removed and stored. The room had a smell about it—one I recognized from visiting nursing homes and hospitals. The smell of death. It sinks into your nostrils and reminds you that we are only here for a short time.

I finished with the tea and sat her cup and saucer on the table, and held mine on my lap.

"So, Jake, tell me. How have you been?" She reached for her saucer and cup.

"Good. How are you doing with all of this? Surgery was a success, right?"

"Yep. They think they got it all, but waiting on some additional test results."

I looked at her eyes. They were distant. Not the ones I first met in this room. The blue had been replaced with chemicals that promised nothing more than hope. "What type of tests?" I asked.

"Liver." Mel stirred her cup and blew across the top.

"Is that something they are concerned about?"

"Apparently so…well, now," she said, "to be honest, I don't think they really know. Life's a crap shoot, you know that, and we must learn to do the best we can."

"I'm so sorry, Mel." I choked a bit. "I didn't know that was something they were looking at. But…"

"Jake, look. This is a tough thing." She held her thin arms out. "Let's not spend our time talking about something neither of us have control over. Have you thought about what I said? About graduation?"

"Yeah, sure. I've thought about it. A lot actually."

"Well…"

"I understand what you mean, and I get it. But, I'm not sure how best to do it," I said.

"Okay. We'll talk that through. I've given it a lot of thought as well. I've had extra time on my hands lately, you know. I have an idea."

"Really?" I asked. "What kind of idea? You going to go with me? You're in no condition to fly. Maybe I can have them fly here."

She laughed. "No, Jake. This is something you will have to do on your own."

"Well, you don't look that sick to me. Are you faking it?"

"I have lost thirty pounds, and as much as I wanted large breasts, they weren't even close to that size" she laughed. "Can't go with you big boy. You're going to graduate all by yourself. Just like in school."

I sipped my tea and waited for her to do the same. "I know."

"How are you feeling?" she asked. "Dreams?"

"No. The dreaded nightmare has not returned as of late. But, I am having a recurring dream about women with thirty-pound boobs," I joked.

We both got a laugh and settled in for our usual talk. We caught up about the families, kids, and work. After the chit chat, she got serious.

"You have kept one thing from me all these months. I think you should talk about her."

I knew what she meant. I never shared with Mel the center of my nightmare. I held onto that one thing.

"Why do you feel the need to protect her, after all these years? I imagine it might be liberating for you to speak about who did this." She pulled at a loose thread in her sock. "What do you think?"

"Is it important? Who did those things to me?" I asked. "Isn't it enough that it happened? Do I need to confront her as well?"

"Confront. No. I don't think that's necessary at all, but for you to keep that secret so buried is not healthy for you. For you to be healthy and to be able to move on, I think it's important."

"Okay. I'll think about it."

"Well, Jake, don't think too long on that. It's possible my days are numbered," she said. "I don't even buy green bananas anymore."

"Point taken. What's your idea?"

"Oh...that. Well," she paused to watch me, "you may find it silly, but I think you should consider writing a letter or journal," she said. "You seem to be at ease putting things down on paper. It might help you to organize your thoughts when you meet with your parents. Several of my patients over the years have found it useful to write down their graduation, in sort of a letter to themselves." She sat her cup down on the table and looked me square in the eyes. "It might help."

I nodded. "Maybe."

"Have you spoken to them about getting together?" Mel asked.

"I'm flying to Texas in three weeks."

"Good. That is a big step—you're anxious?"

"Anxious? No...but I'm afraid as hell."

"You have lived in fear your entire life. What's new? It took a lot of courage to share these things with me. I think you'll do just fine."

"Telling Mom and Dad will be probably the hardest thing I've ever done, and to be honest, I don't really know why."

"Jake, you've wrestled with the fear of fault for a very long time. It's time to get this off your back. Once you do, I think you'll feel a sense of relief. Maybe then, you can begin to repair the damage this has left in its wake at home."

"Thanks for the pep talk, Doc," I smiled.

"Look beneath the butter bean plant, Jake. I think you've been afraid to lift it, and you might find some important answers, if you did."

"I will try."

"I know you will." She smiled and glanced at her watch. "Well, it's time to stop. My movers will be here any second. I hope you'll reach out when you return."

"You can count on it," I said lifting myself off the couch.

We said our goodbyes and hugged for what seemed a very long time. This small, frail woman had given me so much of herself, but mostly, she shared her strength. Mel listened to things no person should have to say to another.

When I reached my car, the sun had disappeared, and the street lights shone bright in the parking lot. I sat behind the steering wheel for a long while and wiped the tears that needed to come.

I needed to write. I would start my journal tonight.

CHAPTER NINETEEN

The Threshing Floor

(Spring 2005)

THREE WEEKS FLEW BY. The voice echoed at the gate and tugged me out of my morning daze. "Ladies and gentlemen, we will be boarding all rows to Houston. All rows, please."

I turned to the older gentleman sitting beside me at the gate. "Did she say all rows?"

"Yep." He glanced over at me and smiled. "I heard it and don't even got my ears on, boy," he said as he pointed to the speaker directly above our heads. After a second, he stood and walked to the jet way, turning at the last minute to wave me on. "What's the matter—you afraid of flying?" He shook his head and disappeared down the dark tunnel.

My plane was on time, but I didn't care about on-time departures or seat numbers, or even getting upgraded to first class. I hoped the airline mechanics would scuttle the entire flight and find some reason to delay or even cancel the flight, or that the unpredictable weather of Texas would find its way to the radar. I even asked the flight attendant about the toilet. I read somewhere that the number one reason for delay or cancellation was toilet troubles.

I waited until the very last minute to board. "Excuse me, ma'am," I whispered, "Do the toilets work on this plane?"

The flight attendant was cute, bottle blonde, and didn't have a clue. The one thing she did have was a working microphone in her hand. "Yes, sir. I just flushed it, and as far as I can tell, she's working like a charm." Her words echoed over the intercom. A hundred heads turned to the front of the plane. Even some guy loading his suitcase in the overhead bin stopped mid-lift to see which schmuck was concerned about the toilet.

"Please make sure your seatbelts are fastened ladies and gentlemen, and your tray tops are closed and locked for takeoff." She paused as she donned the yellow life vest around her neck.

"Are you sure? I mean, you guys can't fly if the toilet's not working...right?" I asked, standing next to her in the galley, dodging the curly cord as she moved about grabbing a seat belt for her demonstration.

"Well, sir, is there some bowel problem you need to tell me about?" she asked, as she punched the microphone to ask passengers if they could hear her. The front five rows all nodded the affirmative.

"Bowel problem? Oh, no. I didn't mean that. I was just curious."

"Well, if you need to sit near the toilet because of diarrhea, I can ask someone to exchange seats with you."

Before I could speak, she was off and running, with microphone in hand. "Folks, we have a gentleman in the front of the plane who's having a bad day." She cuffed the microphone and whispered, "Diarrhea," stretching the word like it had ten syllables. "We've all been there, so let's not pretend we haven't. Could we have a volunteer exchange seats with him? Someone near the toilet would be great."

She turned to see the shock on my face. "What seat are you in, sir?"

I looked down the aisle. It was as quiet as church during invitation. All eyes were on me and blondie, waiting for one of us to yell "Amen."

"Seat, um, 12C," I said.

"Well, it's your lucky day." She glanced at my seat assignment. "Mr. Travis, your seat is only two rows from the toilet." Back into the microphone, "Never mind ladies and gentlemen, a false alarm here. Thanks to any of you who considered a seat exchange."

This plane had thirty rows and walking down to 12C seemed to take an eternity. Along the way, two elderly women offered me pink Pepto Bismol.

"I have a nervous bowel myself," one lady said to me, as she handed me a roll of pink things. "Thelma here," pointing to the elderly woman sitting next to her, "has diarrhea every time we fly. Ain't that right, Thelma?" Poor gal was strapped to an oxygen line and was unable to say anything, but she did give me the thumbs up sign.

I took the meds just in case, slumped as far down in my seat as possible and prayed for sleep.

The Hertz bus deposited me at the Gold Lot. I found my SUV and pointed her north. I had a few hours of windshield time to think about how my news might affect Mom and Dad. My biggest fear was they'd blame themselves, or even worse, blame me. Not the outcome I wished. I believed I was beyond the blame game now and felt a sense of calm come over me as the road noise sang its song. As the cars and trucks whizzed by me, I thought about how all of this affected me as a person. Keeping a dark secret for most of my life is bound not to be good. Of course, my inability to tell someone, even as an adult, really made me angry, and I think that anger filtered through all of my relationships. Was it simply the lack of trust or was I so self-deprecating that I would rather harm myself than hurt another? As a lawyer, I thrive on asking the right questions, but … maybe there are questions that really don't have an answer.

Mel suggested that I keep a journal of my thoughts, and when I first started the exercise a few weeks back, it was painful, but as I began to listen to the words penned to paper, I felt the weight lift. I discovered a miracle—the more I wrote, the better I felt.

Finally, after weeks of writing in my journal, I finished my letter. It was a big step for me, and I prayed for the courage to read it aloud.

Dear Jake,

A long time ago, something bad happened to you. Out of shame, you buried it and found solace in the ways of a child. You felt not wanted and worthless and believed that you were somehow bad or not fit. Shame cannot be remedied through the passage of time, but simply endured. And despite those bad things, you endured.

But, it wasn't your fault.

Growing up with feelings like fear, guilt, and shame weighed down your shoulders. You kept quiet for a very long time, allowing those feelings to grow and mature inside you. You were just a kid, and you were confused. Parts of you wanted to scream out loud. But you were simply not ready.

As you grew older, these feelings slept. I know you believed them to be gone forever during those long silent breaks. No dreams to remind you, but those memories were always there. Alone with your thoughts, they would sometimes wake up and visit you. Those were tough moments, and they made you relive the bad things. Each time they visited, you would dig a little faster, laying them to rest, a little deeper.

I know you prayed for strength to speak out. I can remember the prayer Sam encouraged you to say that day on the bench.

"Dear Jesus, help my nights to be calm and my dreams to be of only good things. Amen."

You buried those things so deep that it took years for them to show their face. During those later days, you felt angry, but didn't know why. You blamed yourself for things that happened and others for things that didn't matter. You learned to exist, to pretend, and to detach yourself for long periods of time from those who loved you. If you didn't speak of those moments, those bad things, they didn't happen. Saying the words out loud would give them life and sustain their existence.

But, it wasn't your fault.

I believe moments change our lives, some good and some not. The bad things that happened to you changed you forever. No doubt about it. The space between you and others grew larger, and you struggled to make everything all right. You wanted life to sit straight, and when life cheated you, it hurt, bringing back those horrible feelings of helplessness.

For years, your worth lay with the approval of others. That is a tough row to plant for anyone. It's why you tried so hard to please everyone, all the time, and when you failed, it drained your energy to pick up and go again. After a while, the load grew unbearable, and that is when things begin to crack.

You often questioned your happiness. Truthfully, you weren't happy, but you learned to repress and pretend. You were an actor chained to a character, suffering a script with no ending. But, you were loved, and the strength you so often sought was all around you. It was indeed inside you. All it needed was light so you could see.

On this day of graduation, I want to remind you of the countless moments with dozens of people, making the man you see in the mirror. Maybe our destiny of whipping pain and hurt is simply to travel with our collections of laughter and love and the people behind them. They may not win each and every battle, as pain and hurt are resilient enemies, but they win enough to make the ride worth taking. And to be honest, it's always worth taking.

Hug Mom and Dad. They didn't have much to give, but you got all they had. That is more than anyone can expect.

Worry less, Jake. There are some things you cannot change. Learn to accept those.

And remember, it wasn't your fault.

Jake Travis

ঔত৹৻ও

The rain lasted less than a hundred miles, and as I turned onto the dirt road, billowing dust welcomed me home. The drought in Texas had been long, and many weary farmers had given up watering. The rental kicked up the bowl as I made the first turn. The bumps and holes wished for a grader, but the county rarely made it this far out.

Slowing the SUV, I pulled over to the edge of a ditch and sat for a moment, catching my thoughts and listening to the engine idle. I let the dust blow past and lowered my window. I smelled the muscadines and wild blackberries. A smell I remembered from my tree climbing days. I looked up and saw the old white clapboard church perched upon the hill ahead. The large oaks, whose branches once supported tire swings, and the picnic tables were now gone.

There were many great memories of inside the walls of the church, not the least my first kiss by someone younger than my grandmother. Gretchen Smith. Well, it wasn't much of a kiss; we were only nine at the time, and if the truth be known, it simply might have been a face bump during hide and seek. My memory struggles for a moment, but chooses to settle on the kiss. She liked my shoes. I was sure of it.

My watch was fast, and I was early, a calling card of mine and an irritant to many of my friends and family.

I decided to pull to the gravel parking area. I hadn't visited this old church in thirty years. Shutting the engine off, I stepped out. The air was still, and the sun crested the tree line in the distance. As in my youth, I could feel God around me. I know it seems strange to think God has time to sit around a country church, but his presence was here as I walked to the front door. I paused for a moment and looked about, afraid that the knob would be locked. I turned it, and the door opened.

Mt. Zion Missionary Baptist Church was small ... no, tiny. The center aisle, covered in a long narrow rug, divided the congregation. Hatfields to the left, McCoys to the right. Down the aisle sat the pulpit, slightly elevated to give full view to its preacher. The old upright piano sat in the right corner. I touched the keys and smiled. Still out of tune. The walls behind the piano held the daily attendance records, the monthly records, and the offerings to date. The attendance last Sunday stood at forty-three; the offering was $200. I could see the plates stacked on the table beside the pulpit, and I dug deep to find a twenty, stuffing it into the middle plate.

I sat down on the third row where Mom deposited me so many times as a youngster. I pulled out my journal. The room was still, and I reflected on the moments from this old pew. I could still hear Brother Thompson, wet with perspiration, preaching his fire and brimstone message. His only message. Sure, there were others during Christmas and Easter, but this church was mostly about hell and how to stay out of it.

"Brothers and sisters in the Lord," he would shout, "we must repent from the sins of the world and take up the cause of the Lord." Mr. Kelly from the rear, suddenly filled with the spirit, would yell, "Amen!"

It was contagious, this yelling of "amen" from the congregation. This flock participation would excite preacher Thompson even more. He would begin to pound the pulpit with his fist and shout even louder, beckoning someone to accept Christ, and do it today. A chain reaction would be set off lasting well into lunch time. During the invitation, I would hold Mom's hand. All the yelling and screaming could be frightening to a little guy, but mostly I was always hungry.

"Momma," I would say, "I'm hungry. My stomach's growling."

"Shush, Jake. Jesus is coming," she would whisper, jerking my arm and giving me the evil eye.

"Well, I hope he's bringing fried chicken, 'cause I'm starving," I would tell her.

The preacher moved slowly and stood in front of the pulpit, his arms opened wide. The piano softly played "Just as I Am," his favorite invitational hymn. I admit, it was a good one, probably one of my favorites. The hymn had four verses. Many Sundays we sang through them multiple times before he finally bowed his head and closed the invitation with prayer. At the end, a dozen men and women knelt at the front of the church…praying.

I often wondered for whom they prayed. Perhaps I was on that list.

Today, there was a new baptismal in the back, sitting atop stairs so the church folk could watch those new to the Lord. In my day, it wasn't there. The church used a shallow creek nearby to dunk its new brothers and sisters in Christ.

I was nine years old when I took the walk down this same red carpet and endured the dip in that gritty creek. That one moment sustained me during pretty tough times; however, I wondered if God had grown weary of me over the years and left me to walk in solitude. I hoped not.

Kneeling in that old pew, I asked God to carry me … one more time.

CHAPTER TWENTY

Graduation

NEITHER MOM NOR DAD KNEW of the reason behind my abrupt visit. They quizzed me time and again in the days before my flight, but I deflected their questions the best I could. As I turned the last corner on the dusty road, I could see Dad's truck parked out front. He was out back on his riding lawn mower cutting the grass. He loved cutting grass, and Mom loved him cutting grass. She needed him out of the house. Since his retirement, he took to cleaning out things. The garage. The attic. The barn. The closets. I think he ran out of places to clean, which meant he was in her way.

Mom banished him to mowing the four acres around the house and gardening. She threatened his life if he tried to clean anything or to help her in the kitchen. So, he mowed and worked the garden with the zeal of a sharecropper on new land. He watched me turn into the driveway and pulled the mower over and shut the engine down. He leaped off the tractor and waved. I heard him shout for Mom, announcing my arrival.

"Jake's here, Momma," he yelled, waving at her standing in the window.

Mom stepped out of the house and onto the front porch wearing a white stained apron and worn house slippers. She was holding a dish towel in her left hand and a black iron skillet in her right. Her hair was pulled up, and her face was flushed from the heat of the kitchen. They met at the corner of the garage and hustled to greet me. Hand in hand.

I stepped from my SUV, and the three of us hugged.

"Son, you're nuthin' but skin and bones," she said, stepping back to look at me. "I gotta get some food down you before you blow away. Come on in the house. Got pork chops in the oven, rolls ready, and just finished topping an apple pie." She grabbed my hand, jerking me inside.

Dad looked at me as we walked up the porch stairs and said, "He needs a drink, Momma." He took my bag from my grip. "Come on, son, I stopped by Luther's and picked up a fifth of Jack Daniels. It's a pretty old bottle too—had dust all over it."

"You know," I said, "I'm pretty hungry, but a shot of Jack sounds like a good start."

Dad held the screened door as we walked in. His overalls hung loose, and his gray hair had thinned. They both were getting older and suddenly, shame came over me. I'd been so focused over the past months on my problems; I missed the signs of age in my own mom and dad. "I might want a double, Dad," I said. "Toss some ice cubes in there as well."

"Done." He sat my bag down and rushed to his liquor cabinet. "Take a seat in my easy chair, Jake. I fixed the handle so you won't keel over backwards." I heard him fumbling with the ice trays. "Since my retirement, been fix'n lots of things I just didn't have time to before. Now, got all the time in the world to help Momma around the house. Ain't that right, Momma?"

I glanced at Mom, and she didn't hide the roll of her eyes. I smiled. She looked frail standing at the sink, washing the dirty dishes. She never wanted a dishwasher. Said it was a waste of good money. "God gave me two hands for washing dishes, picking beans, and spanking kids," she often said.

"Jake, now we have corn on the cob or collards. Which would you like tonight?" Mom asked, as she finished drying the skillet. "Personally, the collards are fresh out of the garden. 'Course, the corn is from last summer, but it's really good, too."

"Mom, why don't we have both?" I said, watching her dash from one end of the tiny kitchen to the other.

She grinned. "That's my boy!" She lifted the apple pie high in the air. "See, made it just for you. Took me all night to roll out that crust." She paused and nodded over at Dad, "Your daddy helped me. Could've got it done in fifteen minutes...but he insisted on helping."

Dad appeared from the kitchen, holding two Mason pint jars of whiskey. "Not sure how much a double is, so I just filled them up. Don't want your mouth to go dry."

"Thanks, Dad." I carefully sat down in his Lazy Boy chair, trying not to spill the Jack down my shirt.

"How are the kids? Joan doing okay?" Mom asked. "Everybody okay? Nobody sick?"

This is my home.

"No one's sick, Mom. The kids are fine. Joan's fine. They all send their love," I said, taking a sip of Jack and locating the lever to his Lazy Boy. I leaned back in the thick chair as Dad began to quiz me.

"Why didn't they come with you?" Dad asked, leaning into me whispering. "Now, son, if you need some money, all you got to do is say the word. I put some dough into that Apple Company and boom, it's growing like crazy. You ever heard of them. Apple?"

"Dad, I know who Apple is but don't need a loan. Thanks anyway, though." I gulped my Jack to numb the noise.

"What'dya say, Jake?" Mom yelled from the kitchen sink, "You need a loan?"

Dad motioned me closer. "I hate to say anything to her, but I think her hearing is getting a little bad." He sipped his jar and gave me the nod.

"No, Mom. Don't need a loan," I yelled back. "Thanks, though."

"Why are you yelling, Jake? It's your father who's deaf and can't remember his middle name."

Dad shook his head. "See what I mean? Some days it's unbearable."

This collection of conversation continued unabated until the table was completely set. They caught me up on all of the gossip in Legit. Who died. Who got a new husband. Who got a girlfriend. The drought. The crops for the summer. The cost of gas at the pump. The Republican Party. The Democratic Party. Mom's Tupperware party. Who bought and who stiffed her on their orders.

I got it all.

As we prepared to sit down for a feast that would feed a city block, Dad chimed in, "Wait. We can't eat just yet. Hold everything. Not yet. Got a big surprise for you." He jumped up from the table and disappeared in a rush. Mom sat there with the look of a frustrated school teacher.

"What's this about, Mom?" I asked, reaching over and palming a hot roll, tossing it from hand to hand.

"He went to Walmart today. Act surprised."

He appeared out of nowhere, wearing a broad smile and holding a large wax paper carton. He positioned it down in the middle of the table and noticed my confused look.

"Did you know that you can buy wine in a carton, like milk?" he queried. "Sam Walmarts is one smart son-of-a-gun." He turned the box of wine around so I could see the label. Mondavi. "I know how much you love fine wine, Jake, but I'll bet you a brand new set of headlights, you ain't never drank it from a carton."

He took my wine glass and held it under the plastic tap. "The name on the label looks Italian, Jake, so it's bound to be good, right?" He passed me a full glass.

"Wow, Dad. This looks great." I finished off my Jack and picked up my glass of wine. "What makes you think it's Italian?"

He looked at the label. "See here. Most wines from Italy end with a vowel. Mon…da…vi." He turned the carton around so Mom could see. "That's what the lady said at the checkout counter."

Mom smiled and reached for the carton. "The checkout counter, huh? Well, I'm sure she's an expert in Italian wines." She pulled her readers on and studied the back of the carton. "I suspect this expert has a sixth grade education, three kids, a mobile home, and never even been out of this county."

Dad passed the glasses of wine around. "What's your point?"

"Says, right here. California." Mom pushed the box back to Dad and dropped her readers to the table.

Dad's face wrinkled as he picked up her bifocals. "That's where they packaged it, Momma. The grapes are grown in Italy, stomped over there in Italy, and shipped from Italy."

I knew this conversation could last well into next week, so I lifted my glass toward the ceiling and proposed a toast.

"Here's to collards and corn."

After dinner, we sat out on the back porch in the deer hide rocking chairs and watched the sun disappear behind the tall pines. Our tongues were tired and our bellies full. It was quiet in these woods, apart from the crickets singing their songs.

"Mom. Dad. I need to tell you something," I said. "First, I want you to know I love you both with all my heart, and I'm not telling you this because I need you to do something." I paused. "But, a few months ago I went to see someone…a doctor."

Mom's lips quivered and tears flowed. Dad sat in silence, his eyes watched me as I struggled to find the words. Mom took my hand in hers.

"Don't tell me that you got testicular cancer, Jake, that seems to be going around a lot these days," Mom said, squeezing my hand. "Uncle Bob had that, you know. He's just fine."

"Momma, you don't catch ball cancer, hun. Like from a toilet seat? And Bob didn't have ball cancer, he had butt cancer," Dad said.

"Mom," I said, "I don't have testicular cancer, and Uncle Bob had colon cancer, Dad, not butt cancer."

"I thought they neutered him right off," she said. "All I know is he wore big boy diapers for several months."

"Momma, he wore them diapers 'cause he was crapping in a sack," Dad said. "It was awful. I was over there once when he had to go." He looked at me and finished by pointing his finger and saying, "If that ever happens to me, just shoot me with my twelve gauge."

I lifted my hand to slow the banter. "Mom, Dad. Please just listen to me for a second. A long time ago, something bad happened to me," I said quickly before they started again, "and I need to tell you what happened because I've kept it a secret for a very long time."

Dad smiled and gave me the hand wave. "Jake, we know all about the moonshine still over at Limp's house. Talked to Sheriff Bevis about it years ago. You and the boys likely saved a bunch of Negroes by burning that thing down. That white lightning can be the death if you don't cook it just right."

I was stunned. "What? You knew about the fire?"

"Yep," he said, pulling out a finger of Red Man and stuffing it in his mouth. "You want a pinch?"

"No. I'm okay. Well, that's good you knew about the fire. But that's not it. That's not what I want to talk to you about." I stood and walked over to the edge of the porch and leaned into the log post. I could hear the quail calling in the distance as the last light of day turned gray. I noticed that the crickets had gone still, urging me on.

"Well, Goddamn, Jake, would you just get to it? Spit it out, son. You're killing your mom over there. Look at her. She's worried you're in a bad way."

I did not face them. I watched the gray turn dark and struggled to speak. But once I started talking, the words came with ease as I recounted the times.

Mom's face spoke volumes. The tears flowed freely down her narrow cheeks as Dad sat with his hands clasped in his lap, his eyes never leaving mine. Emotion was rare with him, but I could tell he was having a difficult time. I told them everything, leaving nothing to conjecture.

When I finished, they stood beside me, and wrapped me in their arms for what seemed an eternity.

I felt the weight lift from my shoulders.

CHAPTER TWENTY-ONE

The Funeral

(July 10, 2005)

THE GLARE OF THE SUN and oppresive heat returned my thoughts to the songs drifting from the inside of the church. I sat in my rental car for what seemed forever. After devouring several Tums to ease the burn left from Bert's Smokehouse, I walked around to stretch my legs. Earlier, when folks began to arrive at the church, I moved my car to a parking lot across the street and settled beneath a large oak tree. No one knew I was here, and I wanted to keep it that way. After a few minutes, I slid behind the wheel, started the engine and turned the A/C on high.

From the cracked car window, I heard the church crowd singing, "How Great Thou Art." Despite the seldom tuned piano, and some female voice eager for a spot in the choir, it sounded beautiful. A few days ago, I believed I could walk into that sanctuary and sit down on the pew next to my Mom and Dad. Instead, I sat in the car and listened. After a few silent moments, a small crowd departed for the gated cemetery, situated behind the church. All heads were bowed, including Mom and Dad's. Arm in arm, the mourners walked the short journey to the gravesite. I saw the green tent in the distance marking the spot. A lone worker rested on the shovel handle, ready to finish his day.

The preacher stood in the middle of the small tent, his Bible clutched tight against his chest. He was tall, thick, and wore a dark suit. A small white flower drooped from his lapel. I watched him greet the few, shaking their hands, saying words of comfort and nodding condolences. He kept glancing at the sky as dark clouds crept overhead.

After a few moments, all were seated in the tent's cool shade, and the preacher began to speak his words of comfort. I watched his arms tell the story of the birth and of death. He spoke of the love of Jesus. He opened the Bible and read the scriptures I recalled countless times before. Finally, he bowed his head and prayed.

With the lift of the preacher's head, each member of the family gradually stood and bit by bit passed the casket, each placing a delicate flower on its top.

As the crowd strolled to the parking lot, I recognized only a few faces—most of them I hadn't seen since I was eleven years old. I recognized my uncle James and my first cousins, Theresa and Kelly. They were both grown up now. I smiled to myself as they herded their own children into pick-up trucks and station wagons. No matter the history, no matter the wrongs, I felt a lump in my throat.

Within a blink of an eye, the parking lot was empty. Several hours had passed, and I needed to walk. I opened the door, stepped out, and began my stroll to the gravesite.

An old man was tending the site. His thin black frame worked hard to keep his pants up. He held a shovel in his callused hands and pushed the fill dirt into the deep hole. I could hear him humming "The Old Rugged Cross" as I approached.

"Hello," I said.

"Beg your pardon, sir," he said, startled. "I thought all the church folk had done gone home." He stopped his work and shuffled over to a dented Chevy pick-up truck. His dark face was hidden under a long brim cap and his pants clung to his narrow waist by an old leather belt. He opened the driver's door, pulled out a smoke, lit it, and studied me.

The gray stone marker was small but tasteful. It read simply:

In Loving Memory

Beth Ann Jones

Born: January 25, 1942

Died: July 7, 2005

A portion of the Bible scripture, carved at the bottom of the stone, was hidden by colorful flower pots and wreaths. As I reached down to move them, they tipped over, and I stooped to right them. The words carved on the stone struck a chord within me, and I stood up and studied them.

Suddenly, I felt a shadow and turned to see the old worker standing beside me, reading the stone aloud.

"Be not hasty to anger…for anger rests in the bosom of fools."

He looked over at me and said, "No truer words ever been spoken, mister. Nope. Don't believe there is." He turned and began to move the dirt about and looked to the sky. "Looks like storms are gathering."

I looked up and felt a drop touch my face.

"You know, that there Bible verse is not what you think." He paused, crushed his cigarette butt under his boot and leaned into the shovel.

"Oh, really?" I asked. "What's it mean?"

"Well, lots of folk thinkin' the Lord was just talking about anger to others, you know? But, I think he meant for us to lose the anger we carry about in ourselves." He knocked the dirt from his shovel blade.

I looked down at his muddy work boots and said, "You've worked here long?"

He smiled a toothless smile. "Just about all my life, son. Been doing this near about thirty years, now. Ever since I got outta the army." He pointed to the casket lying in the grave. "Did you know the lady...here?"

"Yep...Long time ago. She was my aunt."

He didn't move, but stood patiently waiting for me to leave. "Looks like a storm coming. I got to get this done before it starts. Mr. Causey will get my hide 'iffin I don't."

"I'm Jake." I extended my hand. He reached for it, giving me a gritty shake.

"Sorry 'bout the dirty hands. Name's Bottrell. Bottrell Bean. People just call me Bot."

I nodded. "Pleasure to meet you...Bot." I started my way back to the parking lot. I strolled a few yards away, stopped and turned back to where he worked.

"Hey, Bot," I yelled, "you mind if I leave something personal here? Maybe, spend a moment or two?"

"No sir...not at all." He stopped, looked my way and walked a short distance to his truck. He never turned to see what I was doing.

I stood above the fresh grave conflicted with all my emotions. Tears, anger, and relief. Reaching into my pocket, I pulled out the silver dollar given to me by my dad. I gripped the shiny coin in my hand and remembered the times where it shielded me from my monsters. Maybe it was time to let it rest. I took a long sigh, and my thoughts drifted immediately to Mel and the talks in her office, and I wondered about her difficult battle.

I turned the coin over and over in my hand and felt the weight of the silver. Minted in the thirties, Dad called it the Peace dollar. Not for the lack of trying, it sorely struggled to grant me "peace." I remembered secretly holding the coin in my hand as Mel and I talked that very first day, and how it vanished until my next session—the one where Mel asked me to share my dream.

Mel had waited patiently for me to start that day.

"When I was young," I began, "maybe eight or so, I would have this dream. The same dream. Not every night but many nights. I would try to remain awake as long as I could to keep it away…as a kid, I even held a silver dollar until I fell asleep. I tried to think of happy things before sleep, praying that this would take control of whatever drives me to have the dream. I do know it went away for a very long time, and I felt relief or maybe free of it. But a few months ago, it returned."

Mel looked at me and sat her notebook aside. "Usually, Jake, dreams begin to occur at a point in an individual's life when he or she is psychologically ready to hear them. This might explain why they are occurring now. In many cases, a survivor of abuse may not have any memory of the event, but the subconscious will reveal it later in life. You buried this because it was too difficult to deal with at the time. It's quite normal to repress things like that. It's a defense mechanism of our bodies."

"I remember one time I had this dream. I might have been nine or ten. I recall walking into the living room of our house. I was going to tell my mom or dad." I paused. "I chickened out once I saw them sitting there reading the paper. I simply turned and walked out."

"Do you want to tell me about it?" she asked.

"I guess so," I paused. "I mean…I can. Do you think it's important?"

"Let's hear it," she said. "You never know…but before you begin, I thought you might like to have this." She reached into her purse and pushed a silver dollar across the coffee table. "I found this lying on the rug after our session. I'm personally surprised you didn't see it there. You spend a lot of our time staring at that old rug...you know. Is the coin yours?"

"Yes...thank you so much. I wondered what happened to it. I've had it a very long time. Couldn't imagine where I'd misplaced it. I don't lose things easily and felt a bit lost without it."

"A gift?" she asked.

"Of sorts," I said, "from my dad. I slept with it as a child. It kept the monsters away. Silly, huh?"

I began to recount the nightmare that haunted me my entire life.

In my bed.

The room was dark, save for a small nightlight posted in the bathroom down the hall. The attic fan lulled me to slumber, as was its job each night. The fan moved the hot sticky air from one end of the room to the other. The old wooden framed house creaked on its piers, speaking to me all night long with her eerie sounds of decay and settling.

I was not alone. Someone was lying beside me. Whoever it was, she was not asleep. I could always tell when she was not asleep. Breathing. Her breathing was not that of someone in deep sleep. It was the silence of her waiting for me to go to sleep. I struggled to remain awake, yet pretending to sleep in hopes that I would out last her. I knew it was useless, though...this pretending.

Maybe this time.

The walls to the room seemed to fold onto me as I lay on my back. My body shivered as I tried to count the number of times she spoke words to me in the dead of night. I knew the number six. I turned my head slightly to her and whispered, "The number is six."

She shook her head. "No, Jake the number is seven." Then, just before she touched me, she whispered, "Shush...be very quiet. Don't say a word."

I never have.

⇛⇝

Thunder rolled in the distance, and the noise brought me back to the iron bench and my silver dollar. With tears in my eyes, I gripped the coin in my hand, walked to the edge and tossed it into the grave. I heard the clink as it bounced from the casket vault into the damp tomb. I wiped my eyes and looked at the old man.

"Thank you, Bot," I said. "Thank you. By the way, I think you're right about the verse."

"Only the Lord knows for sure, Jake." He looked to the heavens and gave me a great smile, opening his arms wide. "It'll make you free, my friend."

I nodded, waved goodbye and climbed back into my car. I sat behind the wheel thinking of the words scrawled on the marker and wondered what free of anger actually felt like. Maybe this was it.

As I started the engine, the clouds let loose.

CHAPTER TWENTY-TWO

My Last Visit

(December 2005)

"GOOD AFTERNOON," the young nurse said as I stepped off the elevator at Mel's hospital. I glanced at the signage searching for room 420 but did not find it. "Hello, excuse me, Miss, can you help me? I'm looking for room 420," I said.

She pointed me down the hallway. "You'll be entering a different unit when you turn the corner and walk through the double doors. It'll say, 'Palliative Care'."

Illness and death have distinctive smells and sounds. Anyone entering a hospital palliative care unit will attest to both. The smell is beyond the capabilities of any modern disinfectant, and the sound of the machines struggling to keep those behind closed doors alive made me want to turn and run. Years ago when Granny was dying of Alzheimer's in Legit's only nursing home, I visited her a few times. Walking down the hallway to Granny's room, I first met that sound…that smell.

Turning the corner in the hallway and walking through the double doors gave me pause. They both lived here.

That sound. That smell.

Six months passed since my last visit with Mel. She was in and out of hospitals for the past few weeks. As it turned out, this visit would be my last. It was a short stay, and our talk time was limited, as family and friends moved about the room, dodging nurses and machines. She underwent liver surgery a few days before. I don't know what I was expecting, but when I stepped into the room, it was not what I saw.

She was fragile, gaunt almost, and her head had been cleanly shaved. Her lean form had grown skeletal and when I glanced at her feet, she wore the colorful socks I gave her last Christmas. Even they were too big for her tiny feet. The cancer managed to transform her into something almost unrecognizable. Her eyes were the only traits I recognized from my dear friend.

She noticed my glance at her feet.

"I asked Paul to put them on me this morning in anticipation of your visit," she said, with a strained grin. "They are my favorites." She paused and looked over at her husband. Paul was busy moving magazines and books from the tiny couch in the corner to make room for me to sit.

"Paul, no need to move things around," I said. "I've been sitting all morning. I can stand. No big deal."

He paused and looked over at Mel for direction. "Thanks, honey," she said. "Sit down, Jake. Do I really look that bad? You had shock written all over your face when you walked in."

"No, of course not." I walked to the edge of the bed. "You look, uh, great."

"As a patient, I could always tell when you were dodging the truth. Now as my friend, you think you can just walk in here and boldly lie? I am delighted." Mel smiled briefly. I recognized it as hers, but it was obviously unpleasant. She motioned me over to the couch next to her bed. "Come sit. I don't have much time. I have to pay a visit to the X-ray machine in a few minutes, but it's so good to see you."

I reached over and took Mel's small hand in mine and gave it a light squeeze. "It's great to see you, too."

I remembered Paul as a tall, defined man, with a bright spirit. This thing growing inside her seemed to sap the life from him as well. He finished tidying the couch, tossed a pillow and blanket to the empty chair. "Jake, come sit down. I'm going out to suck down some fresh air." He looked at Mel. "Be back before they take you up. Okay?"

Mel nodded and thanked him, and turned to face me. We caught up on family and work. "So, Jake, how do you like Ben?"

Dr. Ben Jackson was my new therapist. He was an old friend of Mel's, with an emphasis on the word "old." He was bald, grossly overweight, dressed like he believed wrinkles were in style, and managed never to be tardy...only late.

"You know, I like him. He's very nice, but couldn't you have found someone younger? I think he went to school with Freud." I eased over and sat on the couch, holding a small package in my lap. "I was thinking of someone, maybe slightly younger and more attractive."

She laughed. "Describing one's therapist as nice is the kiss of death. I could've referred you to Dr. Campbell. She's young, attractive, and just finished her doctorate at Northwestern. But, Jake, the objective is for you to focus on you, not some hot therapist's legs."

"She has great legs?" I asked. "Just my luck."

"So, how's it going with Ben?" she asked.

"Well, he's less demanding, and my insurance company covers his fees in the network, plus he's a scotch drinker. Instead of tea during our sessions, we drink scotch, and I must say he's gentle with the pour." I said. "So, from a purely selfish perspective, I am happy. I'm now a member of AA, by the way. I attend meetings right after therapy with Ben. They are convenient, too, just down the hall from his office. I bet he is getting a sweetener on referrals. What do you think?"

She tapped the top of my hand lightly. "Just keep doing the work, Jake. You've made a lot of progress this year. It's a journey and a process. Unfortunately, this journey doesn't have a destination, and the process is painful."

I dipped my head down, knowing she was right about all of that.

"So, what are they telling you?" I asked. "The surgery. Successful? Did they get it all?"

"Who knows, Jake? After the mastectomy, I felt better, but when the spots showed up on the liver, they put me on more chemo. That wasn't working, so Paul flew in one of his contacts from Mayo. He felt we should at least try this." Her voice grew solemn. "Jake, these guys are trying to buy me time. More chances for moments. That's so crazy." She paused, as a tear trickled down her cheek. "Time is the one thing you can't really buy, now isn't it? Moments are not for sale."

I nodded and handed her a tissue.

She wiped her cheek and looked at me with her pale blue eyes. Paul must have tried to help her with her makeup as well. The tear left a wide trail. "How was the meeting with your mom and dad? Gosh, that seems like a decade ago. Did it go all right?"

"Went great. They were shocked, of course. Mom was afraid that I had testicular cancer, so all in all, I think she was relieved to know I was only sexually abused."

We both got a chuckle.

"Well, moms are like that sometimes." She glanced down to my lap and noticed I held a package wrapped in day old newspaper. "What's that in your lap, Mr. Travis? A present? For me?" She smiled. "I hope it's something with a short life span."

"Mel, don't lose hope. Give it time. You never know what can happen."

"You know, one of the things I adore about you is that you are the eternal optimist. Even during our sessions, you fought to find the good hidden in the bad." Mel paused and looked to the ceiling. "I'm tired of fighting, Jake. I am so tired of fighting. This thing will take me. It's only a matter of when." She wiped her eyes. "And you know what? I'm okay with that." Her eyes grew glassy. "I'm really worried about Paul, though."

I sat there—lump in my throat.

"So, give it up, Jake. What's the present?" she quietly asked, holding her hand out. "Come on. Let me see."

I handed the small package to her. "Here, open it."

Her hands were bruised and stiff, and she struggled to remove the ribbon with the IVs in her wrist. "Would you mind?" she asked, handing it back to me.

I removed the ribbon and tape and held it up so she could see.

She smiled. "Your journal?"

"Well, actually, a little bigger than that."

"What do you mean?" she asked, gently taking the pages from my hand and flipping them. "This is not a journal."

"I have a school friend, who owns a local newspaper in Legit, Hicker Nutt. You may remember him?"

She nodded no. "My memory's not as good as it used to be. I think it's the morphine drip. You should get some of that, Jake. It's really good." She paused and smiled. "Go on."

"Anyway, he has a friend who's a publisher. He hooked us up, and this is a manuscript for a book. Turns out, I can write."

"Oh, Jake. This is big," she said. "I mean, how do you feel about that?"

"I'm good with it and think writing down the story was therapeutic. It enabled me to move on. Maybe a bit easier and maybe in directions I'd never thought." I patted her arm. "I should remind you this was your idea."

"My idea was to get you writing as a way to see things more clearly.

This, uh, is way beyond that simple exercise." She reached for my hand. "Congratulations, Jake. I'm proud of you, and I love the title."

We sat in silence for a moment.

"Picking Butter Beans," she read aloud and turned to face me. "Am I in it?"

"Well, maybe. You'll have to read to find out." I stood and tossed the wrapping paper into the trash.

"Now what?" she asked. "You still thinking about leaving the law firm?"

"I don't know, Mel. But, a little voice tugs at me to do something different. Maybe help others. I'm not sure yet what that could be. I honestly don't know."

"Keep searching. It'll come." She held the pages tight against her narrow chest. "So happens, I desperately needed fresh reading material. I just finished reading *People* magazine, cover to cover. And you know how I love *People*. Thank you. You're a Godsend."

The door opened and two nurses marched in, taking control of the room, moving trays around, turning machines off, looking over charts, scribbling in the margins. "Okay, Mel, time for your X-rays."

She looked at me and then spoke to the nurse. "Could I have just a sec…please?"

The nurse glanced at her watch. "Two seconds. They got people stacked up and down the hallway waiting for radiation like lunch time at McDonalds. We pulled strings so you're in and out. Make it quick."

"Thank you," Mel said. Both nurses eased out of the room. "Won't take but a minute."

"Jake, you have some special knowledge. How people feel. What happens to them. You lived it for a long time. Make it count. I know you will. Do something with what has happened to you. Don't let it all go for nothing."

The lump in my throat moved up. Tears eased down my cheek.

"Mel, you're in my prayers—every night," I said, reaching over and squeezing her hand.

"That means a lot, Jake. Thank you…do you think he hears them?"

I stood, bent over, and kissed her forehead. "I know he does. We just have to keep sending them up." I inched toward the door.

She looked over at me. I read the doubt in her eyes. "I'll read it. All of it. I promise."

As I stood at the door, I said. "You better."

CHAPTER TWENTY-THREE

Out of Time

(April 5, 2006)

FLYING BACK AND FORTH to New York and London on business kept me busy and my mind off a lot of things. I was weary of the travel and the deals. I needed to change my life, but life kept getting in the way.

The emails posted on Mel's progress dwindled to a few quick notes from Paul. A few days ago, I called and left a message at his office wishing for an update. Yesterday, Paul's secretary returned my call and gave me the bad news. Mel asked to be moved home to be with her family. Hospice was engaged in the process.

"What does that mean?" I asked, exiting the building and walking down a loud London side street. "I can barely hear you. Can you repeat that, please?"

"Mr. Travis," she said, clearing her throat, "hospice is designed to give the patient comfort in their last days. We are praying daily for her, but to be honest, Mr. Travis…Jake… it's not good.

I stopped in my tracks and let the phone drop to my side. I thought about the words Mel said to me during my last visit.

"No more moments for sale."

The next day, I called and changed my flight home. As usual from Heathrow, the boarding gate was crowded, and my plane was packed. Worst of all, my name sat dismally low on the upgrade list monitor.

It read Unconfirmed.

I stood beneath the monitor for several minutes hoping it would change before my eyes. It didn't. Finally, I gave up and found an empty seat between two elderly women from Kansas who insisted on telling me about their trip to the Holy Land. After some nods, smiles, and even some "oh mys," I picked up a paper left behind by another traveler and began turning the pages, pretending to be engrossed in the words before me—still nodding and smiling as their story continued.

"You must be a very smart man," the lady sitting next to me said, pointing at my paper and nudging her friend. "Margie, look."

"Excuse me?" I said. "I'm sorry, what did you say?"

"Well, you must be a very smart man," the lady said. "Obviously, you're American, but you speak other languages. That is such a feat. I wish I could speak another language."

"Me too," Margie said, reaching over to touch my arm. "Why did you decide to learn Japanese?"

"What makes you think I speak Japanese?" I asked, returning my focus to the paper.

"The man who sat there before you was Japanese, and he was reading that same paper. Didn't speak a lick of English, though. After Margie and I talked to him for quite a while, he suddenly got up and left. So, are you fluent?"

"Mr. Jacob Travis. Mr. Travis," the intercom sounded. "Please come up to the desk, Mr. Travis."

I smiled at both ladies, hopped up and sprinted to the woman holding the microphone as she was trying to read off other names.

"That's me," I said, tossing my boarding pass to her. "I'm Jake Travis."

"It's your lucky day, Mr. Travis, your new seat will be 1A." She pushed my new boarding document across the counter. "It's a window. Enjoy your flight."

I bolted down the jet way, got my things stowed overhead, and ordered a scotch, rocks. The flight attendant gave me the look. It was only 10 am, but I needed it.

"Make it a double, please." I reached into my pocket to retrieve my blackberry. As I pulled it out of my jacket, the light informed me of a new message.

There it was.

Dear Jake,

Called your office and learned you are traveling. Last night, Mel passed away. We were all with her when it happened. She was so brave.

She refused a funeral or memorial service. You know how she was. For God's sake, don't send flowers and don't make an effort to come home. I think she would like for you to remember her differently.

She gave me something for you. When you return, reach out to me. We can arrange a time.

Paul

The flight attendant tapped me on the shoulder and asked me to shut down my electronic device and finish my drink. I did as instructed, downed the remainder of my scotch, and closed my eyes as the wings lifted us over the city of London.

Alone, sad, and utterly thankful that God had placed her in my life, even for a brief moment, I thought about how difficult it was for her and her family. With those thoughts running through my head, I managed to sleep most of the trip. Upon landing in Chicago, I cancelled the remainder of my meetings and trips, called my senior partner at the law firm, and asked for a meeting.

Don't let it all be for nothing.

It took six months for Paul to return my call. The text message on my phone said for me to meet him for lunch on Thursday at the City Park, near Mel's office building. He was brown bagging it and invited me to do the same. The park was a comfortable place with an abundance of tall oaks for shade. Despite the early autumn shed, the walking path weaved in and out of the trees, until finally, it disappeared amongst them in the distance.

I arrived early out of habit and respect. Taking a seat on an isolated wooden bench, I watched a nearby waterfall drain down stones into a small holding pond. A few ducks wondered about laying small clues of their presence. On my way over to the bench, I managed to step into their pile of clues. I was using my napkin to clean off the bottom of my shoe when Paul suddenly walked up, holding a small brown bag and a bottle of water.

"Jake, how are you?" he asked, reaching for my hand. I stood and gripped his hand in both of mine.

"Doing okay, how are you holding up?"

"Well, right now, day by day." He slid down into the bench beside me. "Been rough without her around."

"I understand." I fell down beside him and pulled my lunch from my briefcase.

We sat for a few minutes as we each unwrapped sandwiches and took bites, people watching. After a time, Paul broke the silence.

"Mel loved this old park. She'd eat out here at least once or twice a week...I really miss her, Jake. I'm completely lost without her."

"Paul, we all lost a special person. She touched a lot of lives ... mine especially."

"She finished your manuscript, you know." He looked over at me. "It was very close, Jake, but she did manage to finish it. Thank you for giving it to her. It was a challenge she desperately needed. She needed something to wake up to, and oddly it was the pages you gave her." He paused and tossed his trash into his bag. "Mel lost all hope in those final months. You felt it, didn't you, when you visited?"

"Yeah, I did. I think she was ready to move on." I took a long drink of my bottled tea.

"She could stay awake only a few hours each day. Like I said, it was close, but she wanted you to know she kept her promise to finish it."

I smiled to myself, thinking of her anxiously reading every single line, wondering if she would get to the final words.

"Jake, you ever wonder why she connected with you, in a special way?" he asked. "Why she took such a personal interest in you?"

"No, not really," I said. "Honestly, I figured that was her way—with all of her patients."

"Hardly. Not even close." He crossed his legs and lit a cigarette.

I watched him in silence. He was in pain.

"I haven't touched these things since medical school. I recall being very happy during those years. Broke, but happy. I thought it might have been the smokes," he said. "You guys had a special bond."

"Really? So, why did Mel take such a personal interest in me?"

"Did she ever speak of her childhood at all?" he asked, blowing the smoke into the air and staring at the burning ash.

"No, not at all. Actually, Mel never spoke of her childhood . . . to me anyway. She even kept you a secret until we met one day accidentally. I got the impression she wanted space between her patients and home."

Paul took a deep drag on the cigarette and let it out slowly, turning to watch a homeless man push a cart along the pathway. He stood, crushed his ash on the walkway, and excused himself. He walked over to the homeless man digging in the nearby garbage can. When Paul approached, he reached into his pocket, and the old man stopped and looked up at Paul.

As Paul placed the money in the old man's hand, he leaned in and whispered something. The homeless man stood up straight and nodded. He reached out and touched Paul on his sleeve.

"God bless her, sir," the man said, darting off with his shopping cart. "I'll tell Luther and Katie when I see them. Dr. Mel was my friend, you know…my friend."

Paul walked back and flopped down beside me. "Mel spent many a paycheck giving out money to these guys. I needed to tell them she wasn't coming back, but that I'd be here. Every week."

I looked at him with such admiration. "Mel would love that." I lowered my head thinking about the talks we had over the past year.

"Look, Jake. Mel was raped when she was fourteen years old by her stepfather. It was horrible. She went through a long and difficult process…for a very long time. She underwent therapy for years after we were married. Not many folks know about this; some of our best friends don't even know. But somehow, I think she would have wanted you to know."

"So, she knew all along how it felt. How I felt."

"I'm pretty sure she did." He reached into his coat pocket and pulled out a small beige envelope and laid it beside me on the bench. "Mel wrote a special message to each of her patients. This one is for you."

I reached down and picked it up. It simply read, "To Jake."

I started to peel back the seal, but Paul reached out and touched my hand. "Jake," he said, "she suggested you wait. Put it in your pocket and when the time comes, you'll know. Then you should open it."

I looked at him, puzzled.

"Don't ask me why, Jake. You knew her. She had her reasons for many things. Most of the time, I ignored her idiosyncrasies. But… the way she pleaded with me during those last days. Tell Jake he will know the right time. Not 'til then."

I held the card in my hand, turning it over and over, wondering what she was thinking. What it might say.

"I'll wait," I said, looking over at him. I noticed he could no longer hide the tears. For a few moments, we both sat in silence, waiting for them to finish.

Paul described her last days and after a few minutes, it was time to say goodbye. We stood, faced each other, and shook hands. "Take care and stay in touch," he said. Then he turned and drifted away.

"You, too, Paul. You, too." I watched him pace along the curved pathway and disappear into the shadows of the tall oaks.

That was the last time I saw him.

CHAPTER TWENTY-FOUR

Looking Beneath

(Christmas 2006)

"AUNT BILLIE IS ON HER LAST LEG, JAKE. I swear, the good Lord's got her on direct dial. Actually, I should call her right now, just to make sure she can make it to her pantry on her own." Mom paused her sales pitch and whispered into her phone, "Plus, I don't think your father can handle all the commotion without you here."

"Okay, Mom, I promise I'll think about it." I walked to the large window in my office. The streets far below me were stuffed with shoppers hustling about for that perfect Christmas gift.

"Thanks, so much, honey. We'll have a great time. See you in a few days." She hung up before I could protest.

"Mom? Mom—you there?"

Christmas was a week away, and Mom lobbied like a lifelong NRA member for a good ole Travis family Christmas. She used all the typical reasons. Relatives dying seemed to be the one excuse she liked most. Aunt Billie was on her last leg, whatever that meant. The last time I saw Aunt Billie at a reunion, she crushed a softball down left field line like Jose Conseco. She was eighty-five when she rounded second base and tried to slide into third, but her skirt got in the way. When my cousin, Taterbug, called her out, she kicked dirt on his shoes and stormed off in a huff, cussing like a sailor on holiday.

The real reason was Dad. His memory was getting worse, according to Mom. His hearing was getting better, according to him. Either way, she was becoming more concerned about his dementia. She wouldn't let me have a peaceful day until I called her back.

"Hello…Mom?"

"Yes, Jake, honey, what is it?"

"Okay. I'll come early."

With school still in session, I decided to travel down early alone and meet up with Joan and the kids a few days before the holiday. The Travis family was large, loud, and was legendary for not holding liquor well. I needed to be agile in case things got out of hand.

The entire family was committed to being there—my brother, sister, their families, and about thirty-eight cousins. My gene pool was a collection of pick-up trucks, campers and camouflage. Some were die hard Baptist on Sunday morning but all night honky tonkers on Saturday nights. There would be Bible thumping and beer drinking…likely from the same relatives. The night needed a referee, and that was me.

A Travis family Christmas, for sure.

Desperately needing some windshield time, I decided to drive from Dallas to think about what I really wanted to do with my life. Life always interfered with thinking about life, and, for once, I was going to give it full focus. I was tired of being a lawyer. The entire profession was boredom, interrupted by bits of chaos. I gave my partners an attractive proposal to buy me out of the firm. It was not

a lot of money but would be a nest egg for a new start. They promised me an answer when I returned after the New Year. From where
I sat, it didn't really matter. I was gone.

As I steered along the two-lane back roads into Jasper County, the
sun was starting to end its daily post. I turned off the main highway
and entered the sandy dirt road that led to my childhood home. The
road needed attention, as potholes littered the worn center tracks.
Two miles ended quickly, and I pulled into the short driveway that
led to the house.

As I approached the frame house, I noticed Mom working near
the barn. I pulled to a stop and jumped out.

"Mom," I yelled. "I'm home, and I'm hungry. You got anything to
eat?" That should get her heart pumping.

She was dragging her potted plants one by one into the barn, protecting them from the chill of the coming evening. She waved hello
and marched toward me in double time.

"Jake, I was wondering when you would get here." She gave me a
big grunt hug. "Why didn't you call? I got me a mobile phone, you
know." She proudly held it up. "No idea on how to use it, but when
it rings, I hit this little green button, and there's always somebody on
the other end."

"Cell service sucks big time out here in the woods, Mom. Here, let
me help you with those pots—they look heavy."

She and I quickly labored to move the plants, some of them quite
large. We secured them in the rear of the barn, away from the large
center doors. During this exercise, she never stopped talking about
the Travis gathering.

"Jake, I been cooking nonstop for three days. I got fried turkey
warming in the oven, a ham bone on the stove, and I just finished
picking a mess of mustard greens over at Bob's. I just made a fresh
batch of tomato relish, with spicy peppers, and I have five bags of
catfish ready to fry up. Got homemade biscuits and two jars of the

best sorghum you'll ever taste. I hope you brought your appetite, young man." She pushed a pot into one of the old stalls. "Aunt Billie wanted me to tell you she's a coming—hell or high water." She looked at me. "That's a quote."

"Is someone picking her up?" I asked, straining to move a large pot.

"Nope. Can't tell that woman nuthin'. The Deputy Sheriff drove out to see her last month and told her to hang her keys up. Her driving days were over."

"I'm afraid to ask. What did she say?" I asked, grunting as I rolled a large fern into the corner.

"She told him if he didn't get off her property right then and there, she was gonna grab a shotgun and fill his ass with number eight buckshot." Her face reddened by her remark. Ass was as close to cursing as she ever came. "Aunt Billie said she ain't never seen a white man move faster."

"So how's she getting here? I asked. "Please don't tell me, Mom, she's not driving herself, is she?"

"Okay, I won't tell you that...but that's exactly what she's doing."

After the last pot was moved to safety, she eyed our results. "Jake, move that big one over to the corner. Then take that fern to the other side. It is kinda sickly. I don't want them crowded in here. They need space to breathe. Make sure we have a couple of feet between each plant."

She was tossing out orders like a drill sergeant bucking for another stripe. I was huffing and puffing, pulling these pots around the barn.

"Sally Bonner down the road," she began, "you remember the Bonners, don't you?"

I looked up, winced, and nodded. "I think so. Didn't she always win the pie contest during Magnolia Festival?"

"Well, don't matter...wasn't even her recipe. Anyway...she says that the county is going to install the Internet to their house. I told your daddy we needed something like that, too. What do you think,

Jake? Should we get the Internet or not?"

"Gee Mom, how would you use it?" I asked. "Shopping? Read the news, maybe?"

"Shopping?" she asked. "What do you mean shopping?"

"Mom, do you know what the Internet is?"

"Not exactly. No. But if Sally Bonner's going to get it, I say we invest heavily in it. Don't want to be the only house on the entire road with no Internet."

I broke a sweat moving the last of her pots and removed my jacket to cool off. "Mom, why don't we talk about this Internet thing later? I can show you how it works on my laptop."

She agreed. "I just don't like Sally always getting the drop on all the new things."

"I understand. You and Mrs. Bonner have been feuding for as long as I can remember."

"Well…she started it, thirty-four years ago. First, I overheard her tell Sandy Billings that my apple pie recipe was a fraud. Lied through her teeth is what she did. Then, two days later, she backed into me at the grocery, and denied she did it. I saw her with my own eyes, Jake. Left red paint on my bumper."

I left her talking to me and escaped to the narrow side of the barn, where we once stored bales of hay, stacked as high as the roof. I found the old push plow hanging against the wall, its handles worn thin from use. My first wooden bird house hung from a rusty nail. I glanced further up into the rafters and noticed my first bike hanging from a wire, the tires flat and brittle. The red flames I painted on the sides were worn to a distant memory.

I heard her voice before she became visible.

"Jacob Travis," she said, pointing her finger at me, "Did you just leave me in there talking to myself?"

"Uh, nope. I didn't know you were talking to me." I lied.

"Who in God's green earth would I be talking to? You just leave me in there, by myself, with me jabbering on like I don't know what."

I pointed to the rafter. "Mom, is that my old bike hanging up there?"

"Yeah, it is. I think yours was black. That's it. Your dad kept it after his cleaning out stage."

"You remember me and Robbie working on that old bike frame we found out at the dump site?" I asked. "We were going to build me a bike. Heck, I think we worked on it almost every day."

She grew silent for a few seconds. "Yes, I remember, Jake. Those were tough times on you. More on you than your brother or sister. You were the only kid who didn't have a bike. Lucky, you were able to borrow Robbie's." She reached over and put her arms around my waist. "Money was really hard during those days, son. Thinking back, I can't imagine how we lived through it."

"Robbie's bike was pretty cool. A banana seat. Midnight blue, with flames hand painted on the sides," I said. "We rode up and down this road, dodging dogs and ditches, on one bike for the better part of a year."

"Your daddy loved playing NASCAR with you both. Waving that checkered flag as he timed each of you for the World Record bike race," she said. "He used to come into the house, after being out there with you boys, just a laughing. He'd say to me, 'Can you believe it? Those kids are out there playing cops and robbers with only one bike.'"

"We were as creative as we were poor, weren't we?" I said. We both chuckled, as I gave her a big grunt hug. "So, how did we live through it? Tell me something, if it was so hard, how did Dad ever come up with the money to buy that first bike?"

"Well, Jake, I seem to remember that you and Robbie worked on that rusty old frame right over there in that corner, trying to build a bike." She pointed to a small workshop area where Dad kept his tools and supplies. "You may not even know this, but your dad would peep through the window every night when he would come in from the fields, to spot your progress. I can see him now walking through the kitchen after a nightly peep, his head down. It's that look, Jake, the one he used to show when he would sit down and balance the check book. He blamed himself for not being able to do more."

"Yeah, Mom, I seem remember that look, too. My arms used to hurt like hell from sanding the frame way past late."

She laughed. "I think you guys lasted two weeks before Dad met you at the bus stop with your new bike." She smiled up at me. "Your little hands were as worn as the tires on that bike. And paint. I never saw two boys with more paint on their clothes."

"So, how did he buy the bike for me?" I asked, my arm around her narrow shoulders.

She didn't look at me at first but kept her gaze on the old bike frame. "Your dad sold his vacation at the plant and used that money to buy your bike." Her voice cracked. "Of course, back then he only got two weeks off. That year he worked six days a week for a year. On his day off, he worked the fields with your grandfather. He really needed a new tractor, but said he could no longer watch you work on that old frame."

She paused to clear the lump in her throat.

"He said years later it was the best vacation he ever had…watching you ride that bike up and down the road until we dragged you in for dinner."

I choked on those words. I could feel a deep hurt rising into my throat. I swallowed hard to keep it from taking me down. Mom could sense it.

She put her hand on mine. "Please don't say a word to Dad, okay?"

"Sure—won't say a word." I looked around. "By the way, where is Dad? We could've used an extra back on those pots."

She smiled and nodded toward the back pasture. "Where he sits almost every evening." She touched my sleeve as I turned. "I want you to be prepared, Jake."

"What do you mean, Mom?" I picked up my jacket from the wooden bench.

"I hope he recognizes you," she said, looking me square in the eyes.

Now I was worried. Mom apparently kept Dad's deeper dip to dementia all to herself.

I quickly put my things away, pulled my jacket on, and hiked out of the barn toward the back pasture. Along the way, I picked up an empty metal bucket and a couple of old, torn lawn chairs, their legs rusty and bent. It was getting cold, so I grabbed a horse blanket off the rail.

Dad was out in his garden. The day was barely clinging to the last of the light, and there he was walking the fainted rows of a garden long since given back to the land. Talking like the garden could respond. Checking his plants for new beans.

He stood up straight, arched his back, and worked the kinks from the daily chores. It was a familiar move. I walked up behind him and touched his shoulder. He turned and looked at me, not saying a word. His eyes searched for some spark of recognition. Before he could say anything, I laid out the chairs.

"Dad, let me do this. Sit down and talk to me. You have really worked too hard today, and I need the exercise." He grunted something and walked to one of the chairs. His worn and callused hands gripped the arms of the chair like it might take flight from underneath him. I looked down, and his tennis shoes were on the wrong feet. I bent down, removed each one carefully, and put them back on, tying them in a double knot. I stood up and placed the blanket over his shoulders.

"Better?" I asked.

"Sure is. I was getting chilly out here. Damn unusual to be this cold in the middle of July. Don't you think?"

I looked over and nodded, taking the chair beside him. I patted his arm and propped my feet on my bucket. "We had a load of fun out here in this garden…didn't we, Dad?"

He didn't say anything, but turned around in his chair for a second, looking back at the house. He motioned for me to lean in closer. "Your Momma put up a Christmas tree. Not sure what we're gonna do, Jake, but why would she put up a Christmas tree in the middle of the summer?"

"Dad, it's Christmas week. Don't you remember?"

"I know what this is all about." He ignored my question. "Your Momma has been cooking like she's headed for visitation." He smiled and whispered, "Y'all are throwing me a surprise birthday party. That's it, ain't it, Jake?" He held up both of his arms. "Don't spoil it by telling me. Lord knows you can't keep a secret."

"I wouldn't do that Dad. But, your birthday isn't for several months."

"Jake, I know that, but your Momma doesn't remember when my birthday is. We may have to get her some pills, you know, for her memory." He pulled the blanket down to cover his legs.

We sat in silence.

Dad's garden was now overgrown with leftover sprigs from years ago and tall weeds from the lack of attention. It hadn't been planted with beans this year. He didn't realize all of that was gone now.

"You need to look underneath, Jake, you always forgot to look underneath." He pointed at the rows of weeds before us. "I tried and tried to get you to look underneath. You had a head hard as a creek rock."

"I know Dad." I ambled over, bent down and moved the bushy weed from side to side, pretending to look underneath. He kept talking about what he wanted to plant and about how he needed rain. How he needed me to help him plow it up in the morning.

"The season is upon us, Jake. It will be here before you know it."

I wasn't sure what season he meant. Was he speaking metaphorically? As much as I hated picking butter beans, I surely would pick a garden full if it meant I could spend one more day with my dad, sitting in our chairs, talking about...well, mostly nothing.

After a while of preaching the Farmer's Almanac and talking about the blown clutch in his tractor, he stood up. "Need to go inside to the bathroom. Those damn pills make me pee a hun'red times a day. You gonna be long, son?"

"No, Dad. Be in shortly. Tell Mom I'll come in and give her a hand."

A breeze caught the top of the pear trees, and I got a chill down my spine, shaking me. Placing my hands into my jacket to warm them, I felt a handful of papers. I hadn't worn this jacket for a couple of weeks, and I tended to stuff loose papers into any visible pocket. What I retrieved were several receipts for gas, two business cards, a stick of gum, a half eaten mint, and a beige envelope. I tossed everything but the envelope into my plastic bucket and examined it in the early evening light. It was wrinkled, had a mint stain on the back, and the ends were slightly bent, marking its long ride in my jacket.

It was Mel's note. Since that day with Paul, I'd kept it with me. I pulled it out many times to open, but felt compelled to wait, just a bit longer.

There was a promise to open it only when the time was right. Mel said I would know or feel it. But how? I struggled with that question for several weeks, pondering her intent. I held the envelope in my hand and gazed out into the weedy field that was once my dad's prize garden. Rows and rows of corn, peas, okra, squash, and, of course, butter beans. All replaced with tall weeds and sticker bushes. The old scarecrow, once tall and menacing, stood bent and saddened.

I spent many moments walking these dusty rows in the heat of summer, picking and talking to Dad. There were lots I wish I had said then. How much I loved him. What a great dad he was.

I turned the envelope over and over in my hand. I could almost feel Mel tugging at me.

It was time.

I tore the flap back and reached in and pulled out Mel's card. I could smell her clean scent lingering on it. I envisioned her writing all of the notes, struggling to get through each one. Giving each patient some words. It was her way.

The card was simple—empty save her initials engraved in the middle. The note was handwritten. Simple lines that changed me.

Dear Jake,

"Life is not measured by the number of breaths we take, but by the number of moments that take our breath away."

Today is your moment. Forget about doing something that counts. Move on. Do something that matters.

Trust me…Don't wait.

With love,

Mel

THE END

Epilogue

The sun peeped through my open cabin window and landed on my pillow. After a few minutes, its long golden string warmed my eyes. They fluttered open, and I pulled the razor thin blanket tight against my chin and eventually, over my head. Despite the calendar reading July, the chill of the morning rarely missed an appearance. This morning was no exception. I lay there for a few minutes, listening. I could hear the roar of the Palisades Creek rushing into the Snake River behind me. The birds started their normal routine, while the lodge's pet squirrel, Rusty, chattered in a tree near my window. It was my wake-up call.

The cabin sat on the edge of a round hill on the property. A one bedroom. Its builder placed a tiny bathroom in one corner of the perfectly square room. I think tiny might be overstating it a bit, but I rarely spent more than a couple of minutes each day in there anyway. It has a miniature European toilet and sink constructed from some type of flimsy plastic made in China. My ass was too big for both the toilet and the shower. Not a good sign. The water from the shower was lukewarm on a good day and a few degrees above freezing on most days. I learned to shower and shave at Olympic speed.

Beside the bathroom door was a small faux wooden dresser. Its drawers were stuffed with my things, but those were of no concern at this particular moment. Atop of the dresser was my coffee maker. It had a German name and was popular with European hotels and stuffy kitchen stores. With all of my years of traveling the world, you would think I could manage making a decent cup of coffee. Wrong.

Pushing the covers back, I sat on the edge of the bed, silently wishing I were dialing room service at the Ritz. "Excuse me. Yes, could I get a cappuccino, double? Thank you."

I stuffed my feet into my worn house slippers and walked over to the coffee maker. As I was searching for directions, I heard footsteps on the front porch.

"Jake, you up?" the voice said. "Jake?"

Grabbing my fleece pullover, I walked outside. The sun was clipping the tips of the cottonwoods near the river, tossing shadows across the grounds. The sky was cloudless, and a slight breeze was drifting in from the north. As I took a deep breath, I noticed the air tasted different in this place— like dew left on the grassy hill. A few yards away, I could hear the sounds of the kitchen coming to life. Even better, I could almost taste the fresh rolls warming in the oven.

"Good morning, Justin," I said, watching him juggle his clipboard and two steaming mugs of coffee, one black and one with a hint of half and half. "Please God, let one of those be for me."

"You like it brown, right?" he asked, handing me the oversized mug. Justin took a seat in one of the two rockers posted on my porch, propping his bare feet on the small table. Justin Hays was the manager of the Lodge. He was young, energetic, dedicated, and one of the region's top fly guides. Winner of the coveted One Fly contest, Justin could have any job in the Valley he wanted. Lucky for us, he liked working at the Lodge.

"Thanks. I was just about to wrestle the coffee maker in the Presidential suite," I said, taking the rocker next to him, resting my feet next to his.

We both rocked in silence for a few minutes, taking in the early morning views.

"How was your night?" he asked. "Sleep well?"

"Like a baby. It really got cold during the night. You may have to upgrade my blanket to something made from wool."

"Today should be nice. Highs in the low 80s," he said. "Fishing report from yesterday said that a 26-inch brown was caught on the east side, near the falls, along the bank, just down from Ed's hole."

"I know that place. Lots of timber along the bank. Tough to catch a trout in that small space and even tougher to pull 'em out."

"That's the place." He finished his coffee.

I drained the last of mine, stood, and set my mug down on the table.

"I'm going inside to shower and attempt a shave with sub-freezing water," I said.

"Okay," he smiled. "The kids will be storming the hillside in less than an hour. Breakfast shortly after that. Smitty and Hicker volunteered to fish today with the kids, so you have the day off. Also, don't forget, you have an interview with the *Times* lady. Do you want to do it inside or out on the porch?"

I was already inside. "What *Times* lady?" I yelled, stripping off my pajamas and grabbing a towel made for a very small human.

"Don't you remember? You have an interview with the *New York Times*." He glanced at his watch. "She should be here in a couple of hours. She sounded kind of pushy. You know how those New York City reporters are."

"Why don't we get Hicker to do the interview, Justin?" I asked. "I'm not very good at those things. Plus, I've got a full day."

"She didn't fly ten hours to talk to Hicker, Jake. She wanted to speak to you, the founder of On River Time, not some editor from a one-light town," he yelled through the screened door, as I walked around the cabin with my hand-towel stretched around my waist, tossing dirty laundry into the bags. "Also, did I say she sounded real pushy over the phone? She would eat Hicker alive."

"I gather she's pushy?" I yelled back. "Why don't we get Smitty to do the interview, Justin? I don't think he's ever encountered New York pushy before." I paused as I looked at the clothes scattered on the floor. "On second thought, we need someone who can string together coherent sentences without the use of profanity. Never mind, I'll do it. Remind them, no beer on the river with the kids. Check their coolers, Justin."

"Okay, I will. Bet she was born in New Jersey, not New York," he said, slamming the screen door shut and walking away. "Remember," he yelled, "separate the whites from the colors. See you in a bit."

"Okay." I pulled my dirty clothes from the bag I had just stuffed. "I get it. Whites and colors."

An hour later, chaos arrived. Twenty kids stormed the hill, each one carrying a fly rod and a large grin. I watched them from my porch. First they ran to the casting pond, trying their luck with the pet rainbows. Twenty kids casting into a small pond put a smile on my face. They were hanging up in the trees, bushes, and on each other's ears. It was going to be a great day.

Within minutes, Justin rang the breakfast bell. The youngsters dropped what they were doing and raced to the main dining cabin, some stopping to remove fly lines wound around their fishing hats. A young girl with freckles and braids screamed as one of the older boys tossed a tree frog at her. A younger, lanky boy with feet too big for his frame, removed the frightened four-legged creature from her back and proceeded to chase the culprit around the pond. No one would guess two days ago, they were all strangers. They had little in common. Some were from cities; others from the middle of nowhere. A few had parents, most didn't, and despite being raised in different parts of the country, they each carried similar burdens.

After breakfast, I gave the kids a short talk about what to expect on their first day on the Snake River. We discussed safety rules and introduced each of them to their personal fishing guide for the day. Justin gave them a briefing on the day's contest for the most fish and biggest fish. No whiteys allowed. Only trout. Twenty heads nodded in agreement as if they knew what a whitey looked like. They'll figure it out.

"Does everyone have their camera?" I asked. "What about your writing journal? Don't forget that."

A hand went up in the back. "Mr. Jake, sir, will we see any bears?"

"Well, it's possible, Jimmy, but not likely. And if you did see a bear, it would be a small black bear, not a giant grizzly. I know you guys told bear stories last night around the campfire, but no worries. These bears are more scared of you than you of them. The biggest thing to watch for when you are drifting down the river is a moose. They will be down low along the banks, in the grass. Lots of times, the cows bring their calves with them. Moose can be rather large and very unpredictable, so watch out."

I looked around the crowded dining room, as Justin and his team of guides started gathering equipment, lunches, and coolers to load into the drift boats.

"One last thing boys and girls," I said. "What is the number one rule in the boat?"

They all yelled it at the top of their lungs.

"STAY IN THE BOAT!"

"What's the second rule?" I asked.

"DON'T HOOK YOUR FISHING PARTNER'S EAR!" they yelled and giggled, pointing at each other's ears and covering their own.

"Okay," Justin said, "you have exactly fifteen minutes before we load up and go, so gather your bags from your rooms and meet up at the fly shop. No running…please."

They darted from the dining hall like they were shot out of a cannon, rushing through the back door onto the porch. From there, they scattered like a covey of quails, scampering to their individual cabins.

I looked at Justin. He smiled and said, "I can't wait to hear what happens out there today."

"Me, neither," I said, walking over to the coffee machine for a refill. After thanking the breakfast staff, I gathered my files and started for my cabin.

"Mr. Travis?" A voice from behind me.

"Yes." I turned around and put my things aside.

"Hello, I'm Jennifer Grant, from the *Times*."

"Hello, Jennifer." I reached out to shake her hand but found it awkward with all of her bags, so we finally settled on a mutual head nod.

"Here…where's my manners," I said, "let me help you with some of this." I lifted a large Italian leather bag from her right shoulder and took her computer bag from her other hand. "You're from the *L.A. Times?*"

"Well, no. *New York Times.* Are you expecting someone from the *L.A. Times* as well?" she asked, growing nervous of the potential competition.

"Just kidding," I said, glancing inside the expensive bag. "Looks like you're a faithful environmentalist."

"What do you mean?" She plopped her makeup bag down on the porch and rubbed her shoulder.

"I mean, this bag is full of litter. Do you stop along the roadside and pick it up?"

She cleared her throat. "Mr. Travis, that's not a trash bag you're holding—it's my purse. I admit that it might appear a bit unsettled from an outsider's view, but rest assured, I know where everything is. Trust me. What you might humbly consider trash are travel receipts from weeks on the road."

Justin was right. She was pushy, but I immediately liked her.

"Oh…okay…sorry about that. I didn't mean…" I motioned for us to walk to the side of the lodge. "We're going to meet out here on the porch if that's okay with you. And please call me Jake." I walked to the tables in the corner and sat her things down in a log chair while watching her wrestle with the big roller bags.

"Remind me again of the magazine you're with," I said, enjoying the rub.

She had a large roller suitcase the size of Kansas and a small make-up bag. But those were the least of her problems.

"The...*New*...*York*...*Times*," she replied, groaning between each word. "Have you heard of it? It's a newspaper, not a magazine. It's out of New York, hence the name."

She paused to catch her balance and peeked over at me. I was smiling.

"Oh," she said, "you're joking, right?"

"Yes, I am. I went to law school with your outside counsel and even gave him some legal advice once."

I glanced down at her feet.

"We don't see many ladies out here in heels, you know," I said, watching her maneuver the luggage, stepping over the cracks in the boards. "Business skirts are sort of rare, as well. We don't see many painted toes either. There is a woman down at the Drifter's Bar. I think she paints her toes. Not sure why, though."

"Surely, you are not serious, Mr. Travis. I mean, Jackson Hole is not in the middle of the wilderness."

"You're certainly right about that. Jackson Hole is not in the middle of the wilderness, but we're standing in Irwin, Idaho, population 150. Take a look around. Closest hospital is an hour plus away. No dentist here. There isn't a grocery store for miles and miles. I don't even think there's a Walmart closer than Jackson Hole. Irwin is not the wilderness, but it's a close cousin."

"Yes, I gathered that from my driver." She let out one last grumble as she worked the bags a foot closer. "He was an unusual man. Spit in a cup the entire drive over. Even offered me some."

"Well, people here are friendly and quite thoughtful." She continued to tug at her bag, with little success. "Jennifer, why don't you just leave your stuff over there by the door? We're the only two people here at the moment. I promise not to go through them, and Justin will be back shortly. He'll take them over to your cabin. I'll just have to rummage through them a bit later." I smiled.

She stopped, grinned back at me, and gave a big sigh of relief, letting her bags drift slowly to the floor. "Thank you, Mr. Travis. I didn't know what to pack, so I packed everything." She started to walk toward me.

"Please, call me Jake. Be careful in those shoes … "

Before the words left my lips, she stepped into a small knot hole in the porch, breaking her left heel completely off.

"Holy crap," she said, stumbling backward and landing flat on her bum. There was a loud thud. Pushing her Jackie O. sunglasses back up on her nose, while keeping her skirt below her neck, was interesting to watch. She steadied herself, sat upright, pulled the heel off and looked at it. "That really sucks. These are…"

"Jimmy Choos," I said. "Nice." I reached my hand out to help her up, but she just looked at me. "Can I help you up?"

"Nope. I got it. No worries." She straightened out her skirt.

She pulled the other heel off of her foot, stood, and made her way barefoot to the chair next to me, cradling her broken heel. Sinking into the chair, she said, "So, how do you know about Jimmy Choos?"

"I wear shoes from time to time."

"Well, if you have a mind to wear pumps, Mr. Travis, this could be a lot more interesting story than my boss let on." She laughed and pulled her sunglasses from her face, brushing her hair back and tying it into a ponytail.

That was my first chance to see her.

Jennifer Grant had shoulder length blonde hair, a button nose, and remarkable large brown eyes—the type that rarely missed anything. She had a single dimple on her left cheek, almost like God thought it redundant to place one on the other. Her smile, however, was her true calling card. It told me a lot about her. While she gave the impression of the got-it-together *New York Times* reporter, she was nothing like that. This lady wasn't pushy. She just needed a break from the city life to gain perspective.

"Before we get started," she said, "do you mind if I visit the ladies room? It was a longer than expected drive and quite frankly, there aren't a lot of places to simply pull over and, well, you know."

"Take a pee?" I said.

"Ummm. Yes," she laughed, "take a pee."

"One condition."

"What's that?" she asked, cocking her head.

"Stop calling me Mr. Travis. Call me Jake."

"Deal." She stuck out her hand to shake mine. We shook. "Hi, my name is Miss Grant," she said, giving me the smile. "I'm joking. Where's the restroom? I'm about to wet my pants."

I smiled. I was right.

"Before you tell me where the outhouse is located, could you please pass me the trash bag?" she said, reaching in and pulling out a pair of sandals. That's some bag she had, and I figured I could fish a week on what she paid for it.

"Go inside, walk straight through to the counter bar, and swing to the right. Can't miss. It's unisex ...so watch the seat. Don't want you falling in—got a bunch of boys here who tend to get in a hurry."

"Thanks for the tip." She bounced inside, easing the door shut, not before glancing back to see if I were rummaging through her things.

While she was in the toilet, I went inside to the kitchen, poured us coffee, placed the mugs on the service tray and walked back outside. While I was setting the tray down, she reappeared, holding her panty hose in her hand.

"Problem?" I asked.

"I don't think I'll be needing panty hose any longer. Plus, it's getting warm out here." She stuffed the hose into her purse and retrieved a note pad from inside the bag. She peered inside and began to dig for what seemed like minutes. She kept at it.

"Are you looking for something?" I asked.

"Yes, I am," she responded. Nothing else.

She kept digging, occasionally taking things out. A pack of gum, a half-eaten Granola bar, airline itineraries, a paperback book titled, Private Emotions, old bag tags, a stick of deodorant, and a small bottle of lotion. She caught me watching her. "Well, you never know when you might need deodorant."

"Agree completely, particularly if you are in the middle of Private Emotions." I laughed. "But, if you will share what you're looking for, maybe I can help." I said.

"A pen…I am looking for my pen." She paused and looked up at me, "Just so you know, that's not my book." She stopped, stood up straight, "Okay…it's my book, but it's for research. I'm working on a piece. Freelance."

I smiled. "Have you misplaced your pen?" I asked. "I thought you knew where everything was in that, uh…bag."

Those words really pushed her into overdrive. I was positive there was a pen hidden in that mess. God knows what else. I wouldn't be surprised if she pulled out a carburetor from a '69 Chevy. After a few more tries, she pulled out a black pen and pointed it toward me.

"Knew I had it. There. See?"

"Good work. Shall we get started?" I stood and cranked out the umbrella for some shade.

"Yes, let's do," she said, looking around. I watched her eyes start up by the fly shop and make their way down to the Snake River. "This is so beautiful, Jake. It truly is."

I smiled. "Yes, it is."

"Let's get to it, shall we? What made you toss away the life of a successful lawyer and start a charity for kids?" She asked, doodling on the corner of her notepad.

"Well, I really never liked being a lawyer. It was a dream from a long time ago. A venue where I believed I could make a difference."

"Were you able to make a difference?"

"No, not really," I said. "The people who needed me cared, but only when they needed me. At other times, I was just some journal entry on the income statement that needed some type of justification."

"On River Time is a charity for abused children. Right?" she asked. "Why abuse? Why not some other need? Diabetes for instance? Cancer? Cystic Fibrosis. The list is endless."

"Well, I guess I felt a kindred spirit with those who were abused versus other needs. Special needs, such as diabetes, have a lot of support infrastructure already; whereas abuse is more hidden. Less open. Something folks don't want to talk about—particularly when it comes to children."

"Justin tells me over half of your kids here this week were abused, and many of those cases involve relatives, parents even."

"That sounds right…why?"

"Seems awful." She paused to look at me. "So, why do you do this?"

I glanced at my watch, stood up, and offered my hand. Her eyes met mine. "Will you walk with me? I want to show you something."

"Of course. What is it?" she asked. "What shoes should I wear?"

I smiled and kicked my flip-flops off.

"Just walk with me…no shoes required."

She lifted her head and peered down to the Snake River, less than a hundred yards away. "Give me a second," she said, stuffing her camera, notepad, and broken heel into her bag and tossing it on her shoulder. "Okay, ready, but before we go down there, remind me why they call it the Snake River?"

I laughed. "Because there are large snakes living alongside the river, and they like to prey on women from New York."

"Very funny." She pulled on her ponytail and tossed her sandals into the grass. "I'm not afraid of snakes. Let's go."

It was a brief walk downhill to the water's edge where she dipped a toe into the cold waters. From there, we hiked up stream a short way, and then across the Palisades Creek bridge, landing us a short distance from an old A-frame house. It was perched high on the hill, with a steep shingled roof, overlooking the Snake River below us. A wooden deck wrapped the cottage, making it the best place to watch for drift boats.

"About three miles upriver, the Palisades Dam releases water to feed the valley," I said, pointing to the river as we walked up the steps to the house. "This is the South Fork of the Snake and one of the few rivers with native cutthroat trout. This A-frame house is typically used by the Lodge for guests. We have four of our older kids staying here this week."

She sat her things down on the deck and stopped mid-step. In front of her were the curves of the river dancing through the shades of the cottonwoods, lining the banks. The sun was up, and the clear water shimmered beneath its face. "This is more beautiful than I ever imagined," she said, walking out to the deck rail and looking up- and downstream, and then at me. She shook her head and said, "Wow. How long have you been coming here?"

"About fifteen years or so." I glanced upstream. "I actually stumbled on it by accident. Over the years, I spent a lot of time in Montana, fishing. One year, I was looking for a change in scenery, and the next thing you know, a decade flies by. Never considered any other place after that."

"And with the kids, On River Time?" she asked, peering down into the water below the deck.

"This is our second year." I glanced one more time at my watch. "They should be coming around the curve soon." I tapped my watch face. "Any minute now."

"Who are they?" she asked, her head turning on a swivel. "Who's coming?"

I peeked up river. "There they are." I pointed upstream. Floating around the bend were five drift boats. A guide was positioned in the middle of each boat, with kids posted up front and in the back. They were casting over the sides like professionals, and as the boats drifted closer, we could hear the guides giving them instruction on where to cast, how best to reach the fish, and how not to catch his ear.

The sight itself made me smile.

All of a sudden, a youngster yelled at the top of her lungs. "I got one! I got one! I got one!" It was the girl with the freckles and braids, jumping up and down in the rear of the boat. "I think it's really big. I just know it."

The guide carefully slowed the boat by lowering its anchor and stood beside the young girl, with a net in hand. "Teresa, you're doing great. Keep the rod tip up. Up. That's it. Strip the line. Carefully, now. Strip. Strip. You're doing great, young lady. Let him run if he pulls down on the rod."

"Yes! I caught a fish. A big one!" she said, looking around at one of the other boats drifting by.

A few seconds later, her fishing partner from the front of the boat yelled, "I can see it!" It was the boy with the frog from earlier in the day. "Teresa, it's huge," he said. "Keep it up. Wow, this baby ain't gonna fit in our boat." He cuffs his hands around his mouth and yells, "We need a bigger boat."

We watched the guide prepare the net, and as he extended the pole out, the fish came closer to the edge of the boat. Suddenly, he reached down and swooped the fish into the net, turning to the rear so she could see.

"Great snag, Teresa," the guide said. "About fourteen inches long, wouldn't you say? Nice fish."

"What kinda fish is it?" she asked. "Please don't tell me it's a whitey."

"A cutthroat," the guide laughed. "A native cutthroat. Look at the markings under his chin." He turned the trout over on its side so they could see and then he placed it back in the net, lowering the fish into the river for a quick drink.

After the drink, the fish came back to life, and both kids huddled around the fish as the guide removed the fly and lifted it into Teresa's hands. "Let's get a quick photo and turn him loose," the guide said.

They did a quick photo pose, and Teresa eased the fish back into the water. Then she and her fishing partner high-fived each other and sang in unison, "No stink in our boat. Got the stink right outta our boat!"

The other boats cheered, yelled congratulations and immediately went back to casting, talking, and laughing. Within a few minutes, the boats disappeared around the bend, carrying the noise with them, and suddenly, the sounds of only the river returned.

Jennifer and I leaned on the railing and waited in silence on the A-frame's porch long after the last drift boat vanished, each of us now resting our chins on our forearms, watching the riffles dance around the boulders. After a few minutes, as she gazed into the currents beneath us, Jennifer turned and said, "I lost my father this spring. During his last years, we didn't get along very well and to this day, I'm not even sure why. The cancer was a long battle, but I remember walking off the hospital elevator the day he died and mounted on the wall in a wooden picture frame was a quote that said, 'Life is not measured by the number of breaths we take, but by the number of moments that take our breath away.'"

I turned my head to face her and noticed tears draining down her cheek.

"I really didn't understand what that meant until now." She wiped her cheek with the back of her hand, her eyes searching the waters for answers. "Like you, I spent my entire life doing things that counted, but I don't think I've ever done anything that really mattered."

She weighed her thoughts and lowered her cheek on her arm, then she turned to me. "This is something that really matters, Jake."

We turned our gaze back to the waters for what seemed a long time. "Now, will you share your story with me?" She smiled and reached over for my hand and gave it a tight squeeze. "I want to hear it all. Okay?"

I smiled back. "Okay, I was born in a small east Texas town in the shade of the piney woods. A place called Legit, Texas..."

Afterword

I have been a clinical psychologist for the past quarter-century. I started my career working mostly with children and adolescents and followed a number of these youth into adulthood. During this time, I've listened to many lifetimes of pain and sad stories and seen the trails of hundreds of thousands of tears. The most heart-wrenching pain in my professional memory was etched by stories of the sexual abuse of children and adolescents … sadly, over 2,000 such stories.

The depth and permanence of the psychological damage varied from case to case. In "better" scenarios, observant caretakers picked up on signs, asked questions, listened, and pending investigation, believed. When abuse was confirmed in such cases, before inordinate time had passed, the victim's pain and trauma were vindicated, sins were named, perpetrators investigated, and many brought to justice. More often, the sexual abuse was unnoticed, or worse, ignored, denied, or disbelieved. It often became occluded by aggressive, addictive, risk-taking, or self-destructive behavior. In their confusion, multitudes of the young victims felt responsible for the evil done to them; some were even blamed or ridiculed for it. All too often, the dark wounds were locked in secret vaults of shame and guilt, not to be talked about for years or decades, if ever.

Unaddressed sexual abuse smashes its way through delicate, youthful psyches like wrecking balls at the bottom of their swing. Innocence is stolen, trust shattered, and fundamental bonds and attachments torn. The damage shows itself in a veritable smorgasbord of symptoms and psychopathology, unfolding for years to come.

Steve Davis sensitively and powerfully portrays the journey of a sexual abuse victim from bondage to freedom in Picking Butter Beans. As with many victims, Jake Travis has the capacity to bury the pain enough to achieve outward success. At the same time, his inward suffering is palpable, and decades after the abuse, the trauma and shame still exact a heavy toll on his emotional and relational life. Eventually, Jake can tolerate the pain no longer, and takes courageous steps of faith into a therapist's office.

Picking Butter Beans is a story of perseverance, courage, hope, and the power of truth telling. Sexual abuse is about evil, secrecy, and darkness. In stark contrast, truth telling flies in the face of sexual abuse, blasts into its hiding places, and turns on the lights. Speak the truth—turn on the lights—and like cockroaches, evil scatters. It cannot stand up to light.

Herein lies the most important lesson to take away from Picking Butter Beans, and the most important thing people can do to wage war on sexual abuse: Face it; tell the truth; and have dialogue about it because sexual abuse is real.

Here is some reality we can either face or ignore: There are almost 90,000 cases of child sexual abuse reported in the U.S. every year; the actual number of episodes is estimated to be 3 to 5 times higher. Also in America, 1 out of every 6 boys and 1 of 4 girls is estimated to experience sexual abuse before age 18. And the rates for boys are thought to be falsely low because of reporting techniques; in fact, many researchers assume gender prevalence rates to be about equal at 1 out of 4.

That means we have to be even more determined and intentional about fighting this war. We need to talk about sexual abuse openly, study it, interview victims, and interview perpetrators. In the past few decades, compared to before, we have done a better job educating children about good touch and bad touch. However, this is no time to relax or rest on laurels. Speaking as a therapist in the trenches, I am not yet confident we have done enough to even slow down sexual abuse.

In addition to truth telling, we need to spend more money in order to adequately wage war on sexual abuse. There is so much more we need to understand about the nature of this scourge, how to prevent it, and how to more effectively treat it. Additionally, the quicker we can get victims into treatment, and take steps to stop the abuse, the less pervasive the damage will be. Along that line of thought, we need to make it easier and less scary for victims to speak up—and victims' friends, as well as parents of these friends. Many other ideas for the war against sexual abuse are out there, waiting to be further discussed, defined, or funded. Other ideas are yet to be envisioned. The point is, we do not need to let the discussion stop or the war be lost or forgotten. It is too urgent an issue. The children and youth are counting on us.

In closing, thank you, Steve, for Picking Butter Beans. Thank you for telling the truth we needed to hear, once again. You have inspired me to continue in this long and important fight. We have come a long way, yet still face an uphill battle. May we remain determined and devoted to make our lives matter.

Dr. Robert M. (Bert) Pitts, Jr.
Adolescent Sexual Abuse Survivor
Clinical Psychologist
Pitts & Associates, Inc.
Birmingham, Alabama

Acknowledgements

Picking Butter Beans is a work of fiction, and as authors do occasionally, I chose to name a few of the characters in Beans after some of my favorite East Texas "characters." You know who you are, and I hope you enjoy your alter egos.

I have been blessed by dozens of friends and family who have encouraged me to see this project through. My loving family, Helen, Eric, and Emily, encouraged me to complete the manuscript and to "make things matter." Mom and Dad, thanks for being there … always. To the countless passengers who shared an aisle with me on planes and trains, thank you for your kind words as I tested my story lines and dialogues.

To Justin Hays and Marshall Geller, and to Bert Pitts and John Croyle … thank you.

All writers are surrounded by incredible people who support the project. The most important is my editor, Jeana Durst, for reading the manuscript more times than she should have had to and challenging me at every corner. In the end, your critical eye made Beans what it is. Thank you … for all the "RUEs" and "YAMS." Mrs. Stovall would have been so proud.

To Dari McDonald, my publisher at Bookmen Media Group, Inc., thanks for finding me and guiding me through the maze of publishing. To Amy Q., for investing the time and energy in this story, and to Michele G., for her editing and proofing skills, thank you. To Sue C., for keeping me on schedule, and to Jorgy J., for mentoring me through the complexity of the internet and media marketing … thank you.

A portion of the profits from this book will go to On River Time, a 501(c)(3) charity, focused on helping young people deal with the challenges of abuse through the art of fly fishing. If you wish to make a donation, go to www.onrivertime.org and "make it matter."

Read on for an exciting excerpt from Steven's next book, coming from Bookmen Media Group in Summer 2014.

Things From a Box

By Steven D. Davis

Things From a Box

Chapter One

September, 2012

The yellows in the cottonwoods and the breeze from the north reminded him that the chilly mornings were about to change. He loved this time of year in the Teton Valley, the sound of the river and the burst of color. Tonight, his cracked dry hands struggled to tie the small hopper to his leader. He hoped his stiff fingers were curses of the cool evening, but he knew otherwise. Age silently creeps up, when one is busy living.

Jesse Mayfield's modest cabin was empty of the gadgets, apart from the tube television and an ancient turntable begging for a needle and a cord repair. Jesse got his news about the world from rumors in town. Mae's Cafe reported the most interesting—who's getting married, who's getting divorced, the number of pies sold at the carnival, and the sheriff's latest arrest list. And Billy Ray's Barber Shop. Billy tended to be dramatic in his reporting, always entertaining, with all the romance and bar fights-- some even true. The Victor State Bank had more news about the economy and politics, which could easily depress even Jesse. But, he preferred Big Mike's Fly Shop for real news... water levels, bug hatches, and most of all, hot holes.

Jesse had owned Big Mike's for twenty years. It wasn't much—an old three bedroom frame house begging for a painter's brush, but it was all his. He named the shop after his long time fly guide, Mike Bean. Mike retired from guiding, but he and Jesse floated the Teton River each season.

Big Mike's fly selection was one of the best in the state, all hand-tied by four elderly widows who grew tired of knitting socks and sweaters for their grandkids. The four were retired from jobs and served as mid-wives for almost twenty years. Victor didn't have a steady physician, so these four ladies delivered many of the folks in the valley. They worked three days a week at the shop, squirreled away in one of the back bedrooms. They each occupied a small cubicle, decorated with a gun metal gray desk—housing their vises and accessories, such as feathers, hackle, bead eyes, fur, and yarn. The old girls approached Jesse soon after he bought the house, and it wasn't long before they took over the place... with Jesse in tow.

Jesse watched the sun cling to the last of the day from his favorite porch chair. He wondered if the big brown was sipping flies down by the falls. I hope so, Jesse thought, as he stuffed his worn hands inside his jacket for a quick warm-up before trying the hopper one more time. He needed his son, Matt. His nimble fingers would get the job done.

After a few attempts, he smiled at his success, rose and made his way to the water's edge. The water levels were down... another sign of September. Most of the water from the Snake River was allocated to agricultural use in the valley—potatoes, wheat, and barley from Ririe; sorghum from Moyie Springs. Fishing hot spots tend to move around during the early fall, depending on water levels and the location of structures, such as logs, brush, and gravel beds. The spot by the falls was his honey hole... hot all year round.

He made a few casts into the riffle and watched the hopper drift into the boulders and then back to him. A few casts later, his old friend came to life, sipping the fly and diving into deeper water and eventually, into the current. This old brown trout and Jesse had known each other for years, but their dance remained the same. The fish puts up a solid fight, but in the end, Jesse had the edge. He carefully lifted him into the net.

"Hello, old boy. Thanks for giving an old man a good ride." The wide-eyed trout looked up at Jesse as if he knew his role and began to thrash about in the net.

"Hold on, now. You're gonna bump your head." Jesse lifted the trout out of the net and eased him back into the shallow water, holding him beneath the water for a few seconds. As Jesse loosened his grip, the brown darted from sight, pausing at first behind a large boulder, then swimming toward home beneath the falls.

"See you next week, old friend." He stripped his fly line in, took his normal spot on a log, and reached into his cooler for a cold Budweiser. Flipping the top of the can, he took a long, hard sip and waited. After a few minutes, the old brown was sipping surface flies not two feet from where Jesse caught him. He smiled. After a few minutes, Jesse gathered his things and took one last glance at the hole. Jessie wanted to make sure his old friend was all right. Sure enough... there he was, feasting on Mayflies with the zeal of a new hatch.

Jesse whistled a tune he had heard over at Mae's Cafe as he navigated the trail back to the cabin by the light of the moon. For some reason, his son, Matt, had been in his thoughts all day. He had not heard from him for a few weeks, but it takes a long time for mail to reach Victor, Idaho, from the mountains of Iraq.

Ten years ago, Jesse tried desperately to talk him out of joining the

Army. Matt was a skinny kid, with a kind heart. He had always been a loner, but Jesse chalked that up to Matt's mom... and the divorce. He couldn't envision his only son in the military, hunting down the Taliban, but Matt was a natural at his job. He loved the structure. He loved the Army. It took Jesse a while to understand, but the military was just what his son needed. After his tour in Afghanistan and a stint in Germany were completed, Jesse hoped Matt might return stateside for good. Matt had other ideas. Two months into his R&R, Matt called Jesse and told him he was signing on for another tour... Iraq.

"It's something I need to do... Dad," he said. "Don't ask me why, because I can't explain it. Just trust me. I'll be okay."

"What does your mom think about this?" Jesse asked, knowing his ex-wife would cater to Matt's decision, no matter what Jesse thought.

"She's cool with it," he said. "She's got her own life now. This is my life. The Army. It's the one thing I'm really good at, and to be honest, I'm thinking of sticking it out. Maybe go to college, get my degree."

"Well, Matty, I like the sound of that... a degree, I mean. You know that you don't have to stay in the Army to go to college. I'll help you with the cost."

"Dad, get real. You can't afford it. Mom took everything you had—this is something I have to do... on my own."

"Okay, son. Point taken. I'll try to understand, but write as much as you can. I miss you, and it's hard to sleep knowing you're often in harm's way. One day, when you have kids, you'll understand the worry of a parent."

"I promise to write. Don't worry about me, I'll be fine," Matt said. "By the way, how's the shop doing?"

"Going well. Lots of orders on the new reels," Jesse said. "I could really use your help this summer, you know. Don't you want to come back someday—run the place?"

Matt grew silent. Jesse had floated the idea multiple times about returning to Victor, running the shop. He missed those late afternoons with Matt, fishing for the big brown and watching Matt design new fly patterns. Matt had a gift.

Jesse broke the silence. "I sent your fly design to Orvis. Bob Thomas runs their fly division in Manchester, Vermont. Says your Twitchy Bitch tested well, and might even get placed in the magazine this season. Just think— royalties from a fly design. He did say, though, they might need to rename it. 'Twitchy Bitch' didn't go over so well with the selection committee. Apparently, there are women on the committee."

"Dad... that sounds super. But, I'll let you come up with a name," he said. Jesse could tell that Matt wanted to tell him something. He could always tell when Matt needed to talk. He was buying time, chitchatting about the shop.

"What's up, bud? What's the matter? You're kinda quiet today."

"Well... I need to tell you something. It's not easy, but you're gonna find out sooner or later, anyway," he said.

Silence.

"Okay. So, what's the deal?" Jesse asked. "You can tell me anything, Matt. You know that, right?"

"Yes, of course. But... this is different, Dad. Way different, and I don't think you're gonna like it," he said. "Do you remember, Carol? The girl I met last fall?"

Jesse remembered Carol, alright. She was from some little pothole town in Iowa. Matt met her at a bar in San Diego. As the lead singer in a band called "Freak Show," Carol seemed to be looking for something, and Matt was it. Good looking. Kind. And never really had a girlfriend. She dug her claws in early and deep. Jesse knew Matt sent her money. Carol popped in and out of his life when he returned stateside. While Jesse never met Carol, he knew the type. He'd seen women like Carol his entire life. Unfortunately, Matt hadn't.

"Sure, Matt. I remember you telling me about her. You guys still seeing each other? I seemed to recall she was on tour or something like that. Didn't realize she was still in the picture."

"Well... Dad... she's pregnant. Due in April. You're gonna be a grandfather."

"Whoa," Jesse said, his mind racing. This was the last thing his son needed—to be trapped in a relationship with a girl barely old enough to drink. "Well...you're right. That is different. So, what's next?"

"I don't know. Guess we'll get married before I leave for Iraq. In the meantime, I'm changing my personal things over to her. You know, just in case something happens to me. We plan to have the Chaplain marry us in a simple ceremony."

"Matt, I hate to ask this, but as your father, I think it needs to be asked."

Matt knew what was coming. There was dead silence on the other end.

"Are you positive, this child is yours?" Jesse asked. "You need to be certain of that, Matt. Did you do the math? Did you ask her?"

"Dad, Carol loves me. She would not lie about this. I love her. And... yes, the child's mine. Certain of it. Now—you happy?" Jesse heard the hurt and anger in Matt's voice. Why didn't he just keep his big mouth shut once in a while.

"It's just a big deal, you know. Marriage, kids, the whole thing seems too fast," Jesse said.

"Look, I know things in Victor run at a slower pace, but I'm not asking for your blessings. I'm just telling you what I intend to do."

"Matt... please... think about this." Jesse's tone was sharp and on the verge of anger.

"Already have Dad," he said. "Look, we can talk before I ship out, but I'm not in the mood for a fight. Okay?"

"Please think about this. This is your life we're talking about," Jesse pleaded. "When do you plan to get married?"

Matt turned away from the receiver and spoke to someone. Jesse heard a female voice. Carol. She told him to hurry up. They were late. "Tomorrow, Dad. Look... I love you but gotta go now."

"Love you back, Matty." Jesse said to a dead receiver.

ॐ∞

Jesse lived at the butt-end of a bumpy gravel road, and Earl Lee, the town's only mailman, detested making deliveries, complaining to anyone who would listen that the potholes were shaking every nut and bolt out of his truck. Earl once wanted to charge Jesse extra for mail delivery, and they had actually had words about it over at Billy Ray's. Earl threatened to sue him, while Jesse promised to beat the living shit out of him if he heard from any lawyer. No suit was ever filed, and they remain friends today. As he approached the cabin, the dusty mail truck turned to pull away.

As Earl Lee turned the mail truck around, he lifted his arm out of the window and gave Jesse a big wave. "Did you catch him?" Earl Lee yelled, as he turned the wheels and slowed.

"Yep, but I think he gained some weight since the last time. I'd say he's a healthy twenty-five inches," Jesse said, waving. "Thanks for making the trip over, Earl. Appreciate it."

Jesse retrieved the mail and casually glanced at it as he walked back to the cabin. He flipped on his outdoor light, settled back on the porch in his lawn chair and began to toss magazines and junk mail into the trash burner. He stopped when he came to a small yellow envelope. His eyes swelled and tears flowed as he read the words in the letter sent from Camp Blue Diamond, Iraq, Staff Sgt. Ryan Peters....

Casualty Notification Officer.

About the Author

Steven D. Davis is a freelance writer and photographer. Founder of the non-profit organization On River Time, Steven's writing and photography serve to promote and provide income in support of this organization's missions. While Steven is an insurance broker by trade, his passion lies in his writing, photography, On River Time, and most of all, family.

CPSIA information can be obtained at www.ICGtesting.com
Printed in the USA
LVOW12s1828071213

364314LV00004B/8/P